The Source® for Aph

by Lisa Arnold

Skill	Ages
■ receptive language ■ reading comprehension ■ expressive language	■ adults

Evidence-Based Practice

- There is evidence that individuals with aphasia who receive speech and language treatment have significantly better outcomes than those individuals with aphasia who do not receive treatment (Hickin, Best, Herbert, Howard, & Osborn, 2003).

- Evidence exists for the effectiveness of several forms of cognitive rehabilitation for people with stroke (remediation of language and perception after left and right hemisphere stroke, respectively) and traumatic brain injury (remediation of attention, memory, functional communication, and executive functioning) (Cicerone et al., 2000).

- Research suggests that, depending on the client's needs, aphasia treatment should target single word auditory processing, spoken word production, single word reading, single word writing, sentence processing, gesture, and using a communication book. Intervention should strive to minimize communication impairment, address emotional health, and facilitate participation in the individual's social context and community (RCSLT, 2005).

- The training of general and specific personal compensatory strategies is an important functional approach to cognitive-communication intervention (Hartley, 1995).

- Individuals with aphasia can often overcome word retrieval difficulties if the listener supplies them with a simple cue. Cueing hierarchies may be useful for individuals with a variety of naming impairments (Raymer, 2005).

The Source for Aphasia Therapy incorporates these principles and is also based on expert professional practice.

References

Cicerone, K., Dahlberg, C., Kalmar, K., Langenbahn, D., Malec, J., Bergquist, T., et al. (2000). Evidence-based cognitive rehabilitation: Recommendations for clinical practice. *Archives of Physical Medicine & Rehabilitation, 81*(12), 1596-1615.

Hartley, L.L. (1995). *Cognitive-Communicative abilities following brain injury: A functional approach.* San Diego: Singular Publishing Group, Inc.

Hickin, J., Best, W., Herbert, R., Howard, D., & Osborn, F. (2003). *Therapy for word finding difficulties in aphasia: Measuring the impact on real-life communication.* Proceedings of the Fifth European Congress of CPLOL.

Raymer, A.M. (2005). Naming and word-retrieval problems. In L.L. LaPointe (Ed.), *Aphasia and related neurogenic language disorders* (3rd ed.). New York: Thieme.

Royal College of Speech and Language Therapists (RCSLT). (2005). *Clinical guidelines for speech and language therapists.* Retrieved March 27, 2009 from www.rcslt.org/resources/RCSLT_Clinical_Guidelines.pdf

LinguiSystems®

LinguiSystems, Inc.
3100 4th Avenue
East Moline, IL 61244
800-776-4332

FAX: 800-577-4555
Email: service@linguisystems.com
Web: linguisystems.com

Printed in the U.S.A.
ISBN 10: 0-7606-0350-2
ISBN 13: 978-0-7606-0350-5

About the Author

Lisa A. Arnold, M.Ed., CCC/SLP, received her undergraduate and graduate training at the University of Georgia, Athens, Georgia. She has worked in a variety of settings including a community speech and hearing center, acute and rehabilitation hospitals, public school systems, private practice, and home health care agencies. She currently works as a speech-language pathologist in Henry County Public Schools in McDonough, Georgia. Lisa has over ten years experience in long-term care settings.

The Source for Aphasia Therapy is Lisa's fifth publication with LinguiSystems. She is also the author of *The Long Term Care Companion, The Source for Neuro Rehab, The Card Source for Neuro Rehab* (discontinued), and *Co-Treat with Confidence: Adults*.

Table of Contents

Introduction

Aphasia is a language impairment caused by a neurological insult. The insult usually results from either a cerebrovascular accident (a *stroke*) or from a traumatic brain injury. We think of aphasia as an acquired impairment caused by neurological damage, rather than a congenital disorder.

Aphasia is often extremely frustrating for the client and his family/caregivers. The client suffers because he has a decreased functional system of communication. And because of this language breakdown, many family members feel their loved ones are now becoming mentally ill or senile. This could not be further from the truth. From my years of experience dealing with clients suffering from psychosis and dementia, I've learned that aphasia often does *not* mimic these other neurological impairments. Aphasia resulting from stroke in the absence of any previous neurological difficulties such as dementia, is usually free of any memory or cognitive impairment. Simply stated, aphasia is a *language* disorder.

As a language disorder, asphasia can affect different aspects of language. For example, a client might experience a receptive aphasia which impacts comprehension of spoken and written language, while an expressive aphasia affects a client's ability to produce spoken and written language. *The Source for Aphasia Therapy* covers receptive language skills, reading comprehension skills, and expressive language skills. The receptive and expressive sections deal heavily with spoken language, while the reading comprehension section, naturally, contains activities designed to increase reading single letters, words, sentences, and paragraphs.

I've written this book as a therapy guide with the most important remediation activities for easing receptive and expressive aphasia. As clinicians, we must often prioritize our treatment programs for aphasic clients. In other words, we need to identify and remediate the most important and functional areas first, then move to higher level treatments such as writing. I believe that a client who undergoes the kind of aphasia therapy offered in this book is not "relearning" language. Rather he is *reminding* the brain of language that is still there in the neurological center. The language just needs nudging and cueing to resurface.

The Source for Aphasia Therapy is packed with functional tasks and simple compensatory techniques. The activities are easy and inexpensive enough to teach them to the client's family members, caregivers, and even friends. These strategies are vital for successful aphasia therapy and are meant to be used until independence is reached, or until the client/caregivers are effectively using functional strategies and cueing mechanisms.

Throughout the the book, the pronouns *he* and *him* are used to refer to the client merely for the sake of the book's consistency. Of course the book is for female as well as male clients.

A final note: As speech-language pathologists, we play a crucial role in educating family members and caregivers about aphasia. We are advocates for the client because we are often the professionals who best understand his plight and frustration. Treat aphasic clients with dignity and respect. Educate family members and caregivers about aphasia. I urge you to use your role wisely.

Receptive Language

The importance of strong receptive language skills is not always recognized by clients, caregivers or, sometimes even speech-language pathologists. When a client experiences a receptive aphasia, the starting point of therapy should address this impairment in comprehension.

It's often difficult to define receptive language to clients and their caregivers. I've found that using words like "understanding" or "comprehension" to describe receptive language functions, seems to convey a clearer meaning of your therapy focus to others. Because receptive language is not visible like expressive communication, family members or caregivers may become confused regarding the SLP's remediation tactics. It's your obligation to educate these individuals and assure them that expressive communication will also be remediated, but that receptive language skills simply cannot be ignored.

The activities in this section provide a wide range of stimulus items designed to increase receptive language in the aphasic client. It is vital to begin these therapy approaches at a level appropriate for the client and to continue with that level from activity to activity. Eventually, the client should reach a plateau where skill levels stabilize and further improvement is unlikely. Work closely with other disciplines (PT, OT, RN, Activities, etc.) to discover what receptive language difficulties are most frustrating for the client and staff members.

I've tried to devise user-friendly activities that require little or no preparation for the clinician. You will also note that the number of stimulus items for most activities is large. Most of your clients will need to practice a skill over and over before proficiency is gained. We all become bored using the same items over and over. Enjoy the variety.

As a therapist, I've been in your shoes. I've used other receptive language workbooks that seemed to just miss the mark. I hope that using these receptive language activities will provide clients with steady success and clinicians with the opportunity to watch that incredible transformation.

Goal: The client will increase auditory comprehension/receptive language skills to within functional limits for imitating common gestures.

Instructions: Perform each gesture. Then ask the client to imitate you and also have him say a word associated with the gesture, such as *wave*, *hi*, or *goodbye*. Present happy facial expressions and comfortable body language as your primary mode of communication. Don't give a lot of commands because excessive verbalizations to a client who understands very little spoken language might frighten or frustrate him. Tell the client, "Just do what I do."

Compensatory Strategies:
- Use hand-over-hand assistance to guide the client if he seems confused and doesn't understand that he needs to imitate your gestures.

- Use index cards with single words or short phrases associated with the gestures to provide additional visual cues.

- Pair movement with music if the client enjoys this type of therapeutic intervention. Occasionally a client's comprehension of written language is much better than his comprehension of spoken language.

Activity: Perform these common gestures and ask the client to model or imitate them. Verbalize the command as you perform it.

1. Smile.
2. Wave hello.
3. Cross your arms.
4. Cover your eyes with your hands.
5. Open your mouth widely as if surprised.
6. Close your eyes.
7. Hold your nose as if something smells bad.
8. Hold your forehead as if you have a bad headache.
9. Place your hands on your hips as if you are angry.
10. Clap your hands.
11. Stick out your tongue.
12. Kiss your hand.
13. Nod your head as if agreeing.
14. Shake your head from side to side.
15. Place your finger over your mouth as if to say, "shhh."

Imitating Gestures with Objects

Goal: The client will increase auditory comprehension/receptive language skills to within functional limits for imitating common gestures.

Instructions: Fill a grocery bag with the following functional items or common items available to you: cup, spoon, bowl, pencil, paper, hairbrush, comb, washcloth, toothbrush, lipstick/lip balm (client's), lotion, napkin, toothpicks, dental floss, hand mirror, watch, magazine, and hat or ball cap. You can usually find these items in the client's hospital room. Place each object one at a time on the client's hospital table. Model the appropriate gesture with the object and ask the client to imitate your gesture. Verbalize the command as you model the gesture, and say it again as the client imitates the gesture. Increasing verbalizations helps the client make associations between spoken commands and gestures.

Compensatory Strategies:
- Use hand-over-hand assistance to mold the client's bodily movements into appropriate actions if necessary.

- Use index cards as written, visual cues. Fold the cards and place them on the client's portable dining table in his hospital room.

Activity: Perform these common gestures and ask the client to model or imitate them. Verbalize the command as you perform it.

1. Drink from a cup.
2. Eat with a spoon and bowl.
3. Write with a pencil and paper.
4. Brush or comb your hair.
5. Wipe your face with a washcloth.
6. Brush your teeth.
7. Put on lipstick or lip balm.
8. Put on lotion.
9. Wipe your mouth with a napkin.
10. Pick your teeth with a toothpick.
11. Floss your teeth with dental floss.
12. Hold up a hand mirror to see your face.
13. Look at a watch for the time.
14. Open a magazine and thumb through the pages.
15. Put on a hat or ball cap.

Goal: The client will increase auditory comprehension and receptive language to within functional limits for following gestural commands during various activities throughout the day.

Instructions: In this activity, you will perform common gestures, and the client will model your gestures. It's best to do this activity when the client either grooms himself or performs therapeutic activities. Keep verbalizations to a minimum. The listed activities are suggestions. Feel free to substitute common gestures that are more appropriate to you or your client.

Compensatory Strategies:
- Repeat gestures as necessary (especially for low-level clients).

- Use hand-over-hand assistance if needed.

- Keep objects appropriate to the activity nearby. For example, have the toothbrush and toothpaste right in front of the client for the first activity. Sometimes just seeing the object serves as an automatic cue.

- Teach this activity to other caregivers involved with the client.

Activity: Perform these gestures and ask the client to model them.
1. Brush your teeth.
2. Brush your hair.
3. Eat.
4. Drink.
5. Wash your face or hands.
6. Sit up in bed.
7. Raise an arm.
8. Raise a leg.
9. Sit down.
10. Lean forward.
11. Dry your hands.
12. Rest.
13. Stand up.
14. Look up at the ceiling.
15. Turn around.

Goal: The client will increase the ability to follow single-stage commands to 80-90% accuracy.

Instructions: Give the client each command and ask him to do exactly what you say. Tell him you're trying to work on his ability to understand simple directions. Explain that this type of task will help him follow directions in other settings such as physical therapy and/or special events and activities.

Compensatory Strategies:
- Repeat the command as necessary.

- If a client is functioning at a very low level, you may need to physically demonstrate the command. As you progress with this type of client, decrease the physical cue to a strictly verbal one.

- For clients who can read some words, you can use index cards with written commands to augment the verbal commands.

Activity: Give the commands to the client and ask him to follow them.

1. Look up at the ceiling.
2. Look out the window.
3. Point to the door.
4. Place your hand on your stomach.
5. Open your mouth.
6. Stick out your tongue.
7. Clap your hands.
8. Put your hands over your ears.
9. Point to the light.
10. Raise your arm up high.
11. Cross your arms.
12. Close your eyes.
13. Point to the floor.
14. Put your hand on top of your head.
15. Snap your fingers.

Goal: The client will increase the ability to follow single-stage commands to 80-90% accuracy.

Instructions: Place the following objects in a large plastic bowl or tub: pencil, pen, car keys, spoon, notepad, envelope, dollar bill, quarter, blank check, and greeting card. Ask the client to retrieve an item, take it out of the tub, and place it on the table. After all items have been taken out, ask the client to place the items back in the tub, one at a time, following your command.

Compensatory Strategies:
- Use gestures to accompany verbal commands.

- Repeat the command as necessary.

- Write the name of each object on an index card if the client responds better to this therapy.

Activity: Ask the client to follow these commands.

1. Take out the pencil.
2. Pick up the pen.
3. Get the car keys.
4. Take out the spoon.
5. Get the notepad.
6. Pick up the envelope.
7. Give me the dollar bill.
8. Get the quarter.
9. Pick up the check.
10. Get out the greeting card.
11. Place the quarter in the tub.
12. Put the dollar bill in the tub.
13. Put the check in the tub.
14. Place the pencil in the tub.
15. Put the spoon in the tub.
16. Place the notepad in the tub.
17. Put the pen in the tub.
18. Put the greeting card in the tub.
19. Place the envelope in the tub.
20. Place the car keys in the tub.

Two-Stage Commands

Goal: The client will increase the ability to follow two-stage commands to 80-90% accuracy.

Instructions: Gather the following pairs of objects: envelope/card, pencil/notepad, pen/pencil, spoon/bowl, cup/tea bag, quarter/dollar bill, blank check/pen, fork/knife, toothpaste/toothbrush, and hairbrush/comb. Place all objects in front of the client randomly, so that no correct pair is together. Ask the client to find and pick up a *correct* pair. Following each trial, replace the objects randomly on the table.

Compensatory Strategies:
- Use gestures to accompany verbal commands if needed.
- Repeat the command as necessary.
- Write the name of each object on an index card if the client responds better to this therapy.

Activity: Ask the client to follow these two-stage commands.

1. Pick up the envelope and the card.
2. Pick up the pencil and the notepad.
3. Pick up the pen and the pencil.
4. Pick up the spoon and the bowl.
5. Pick up the cup and the tea bag.
6. Pick up the quarter and the dollar bill.
7. Pick up the check and the pen.
8. Pick up the fork and the knife.
9. Pick up the toothpaste and the toothbrush.
10. Pick up the hairbrush and the comb.
11. Pick up the tea bag and the cup.
12. Pick up the bowl and the spoon.
13. Pick up the pencil and the pen.
14. Pick up the notepad and the pencil.
15. Pick up the card and the envelope.
16. Pick up the comb and the hairbrush.
17. Pick up the toothbrush and the toothpaste.
18. Pick up the knife and the fork.
19. Pick up the pen and the check.
20. Pick up the dollar bill and the quarter.

Goal: The client will increase the ability to follow two-stage commands to 80-90% accuracy.

Instructions: In this activity, you are helping the client move from dealing with objects to dealing with pictures. Polaroid® photographs are a great way to make the transition between a real object and a black and white line drawing. Take photos of at least 20 functional objects in the client's environment, for example: soap, washcloth, toothbrush, towel, TV, etc. (You can also get some ideas for objects from the Core Vocabulary Pictures on pages 22 and 23.) Place the photos on a table in front of the client. Tell him you will ask him to point to *two* pictures at a time in the order that you tell him. Tell him not to point until you say, "Go." After each trial, move the pictures to various locations for variety.

Compensatory Strategies:
- Repeat commands as necessary.

- Label each photo with a single written word on the back.

- Review each photograph with the client before the activity begins and verbally identify each photo if necessary. If a client is having trouble, start the activity with a visual field of 10 pictures and work your way up to 20.

Activity: Take 20 photographs and lay them out randomly in front of the client. Ask him to identify pictures *two at a time*. Use photos of objects that are appropriate and convenient for your situation.

Body Part Identification

Goal: The client will increase awareness of body parts and their positions in space and identify specific body parts to 80-90% accuracy.

Instructions: Stand the client in front of a body-length mirror so he can see his entire body. Repeat the commands and have the client identify the body parts on his own body. Tell him that right and left is reversed in a mirror. Explain that the activity will get harder as it progresses.

Compensatory Strategies:
- Point to parts on your own body if this helps.

- Guide the client's hand to point to each body part.

- If the client is having trouble with the right/left aspect of the last few items, don't frustrate him by continuing with this difficult task until you've come up with some specific compensatory strategies. If the mirror confuses him, don't use it.

Activity: Have the client identify the following body parts on his own body while standing in front of a mirror.

1. Point to your head.
2. Point to a foot.
3. Point to your stomach.
4. Point to a shoulder.
5. Point to a leg.
6. Point to your nose.
7. Point to a knee.
8. Show me an ankle.
9. Show me a wrist.
10. Point to your neck.
11. Point to your waist.
12. Point to an eyebrow.
13. Show me a thigh.
14. Show me an eye.
15. Point to your hair.
16. Point to a hand.
17. Point to some toes.
18. Show me a hip.
19. Point to some fingers.
20. Point to your left eye.
21. Point to your forehead.
22. Show me a cheek.
23. Show me an ear.
24. Show me your chest.
25. Point to a thumb.
26. Show me your left ear.
27. Show me your right hand.
28. Point to your right leg.
29. Point to your left cheek.
30. Point to your right eye.
31. Show me your left leg.
32. Show me your right knee.
33. Point to your right elbow.
34. Point to your right ear.
35. Show me your left foot.
36. Show me your right thumb.
37. Show me your right cheek.
38. Point to your left hip.
39. Point to your left knee.
40. Show me your right foot.

Body Part Identification

Goal: The client will increase awareness of body parts and their positions in space and identify specific body parts to 80-90% accuracy.

Instructions: Show the client the pictures of the face on page 16 and of the body on page 17. Tell him you will name specific body parts and that he will point to each one you name. Explain that the activity will get harder as it progresses. Repeat commands when necessary.

Compensatory Strategies:
- If necessary, point to the actual part on yourself or the client as you give the verbal command.
- Write the name of each body part on a cue card.

Activity: Name a body part and ask the client to point to the named part on one of the pictures. Start each command with the phrase, "Point to the chin," or "Show me the leg." Increase the difficulty of the activity by naming more specific parts; for example, "Show me the right leg."

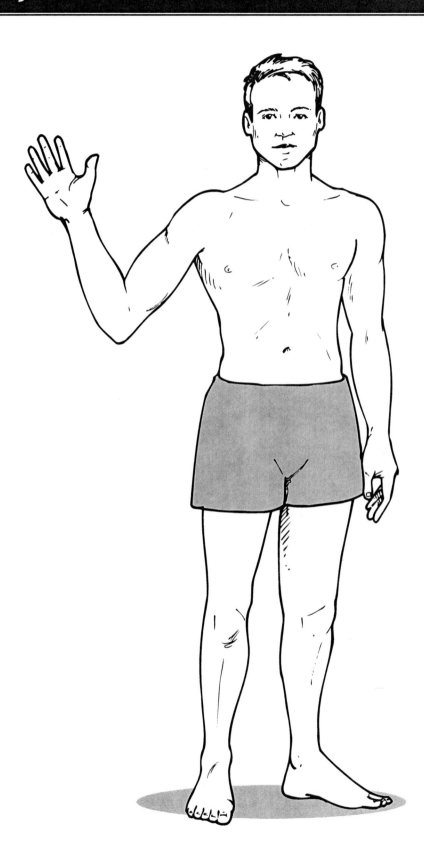

Goal: The client will increase awareness of body parts and their positions in space and identify specific body parts to 80-90% accuracy.

Instructions: Photocopy the face and body diagrams on pages 18 and 19. Cut out the body parts along the perforated lines and place the parts randomly in front of the client. Name a body part. Ask the client to pick up each part and put the parts together to form a face or body.

Compensatory Strategies:
- If the client is having trouble constructing the face or body because the pieces are too small or are unrecognizable, point with a pencil to certain parts or start with easily identifiable parts like the eyes and hair.

Activity: Cut up the following two diagrams and lay out the parts randomly in front of the client. Name a body part. Have the client pick up the correct one and ask him to put the parts together to make a complete person. Then ask him to put each body part picture into an envelope as you name it.

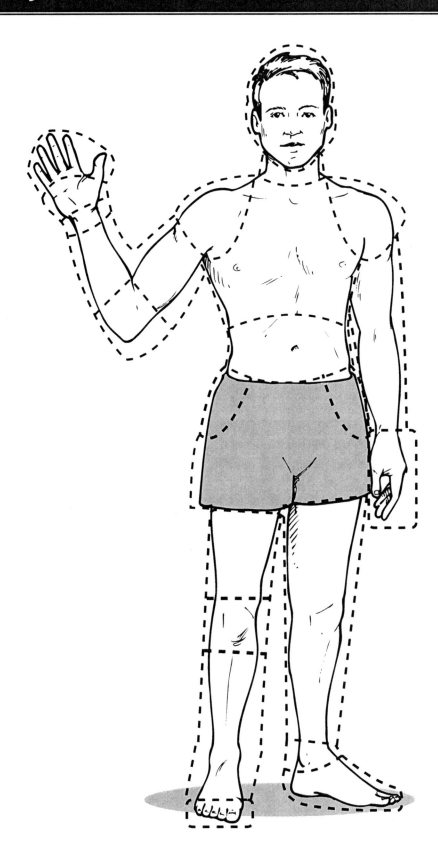

The Source for Aphasia Therapy   19

Goal: The client will increase auditory comprehension to 90% accuracy for object identification in gradually increasing visual fields.

Instructions: Gather some common, functional objects like a toothbrush, towel, comb, etc., or some that are based on the Core Vocabulary Pictures on pages 22 and 23 (not the pictures themselves). Start the activity by putting two objects in front of the client. Name one of the objects and ask him to pick up the correct one. Once the client reaches 90% accuracy in a visual field of two objects, progress to four, six, eight objects, etc.

Compensatory Strategies:

- Repeat the target word if necessary.

- If the client doesn't understand the target word or can't correctly identify the object, guide his hand to the correct object as you repeat the word slowly as many times as needed.

- For some lower-level clients, name *both* objects before naming the targeted object.

- Take into account any visual field neglect.

- Vary the positions of the objects to compensate for any visual impairment. For example, there are a variety of configurations you can experiment with: straight-line, circular, square, right-sided, and left-sided.

Activity: Place two objects in front of the client. Name one and ask him to choose the one you named. Progress to four, six, and eight objects if appropriate.

Goal: The client will increase auditory comprehension to 90% accuracy for picture identification in gradually increasing visual fields.

Instructions: Photocopy the Core Vocabulary Pictures on pages 22 and 23. Choose appropriate pictures. Cut out the pictures you'll use. As in the Object Identification activity on page 20, start this activity by placing two pictures in front of the client. Name one and ask him to point to the correct one. When the client reaches 90% accuracy in a visual field of two, move to four, six, and eight pictures, until you find his maximum visual field for the activity.

Compensatory Strategies:
- For some lower-level clients, name *both* objects before naming the targeted object.

- If the client doesn't understand the target word or can't correctly identify the object, guide his hand to the correct object as you repeat the word slowly as many times as needed.

- Consider possible visual difficulties or visual neglect. Reduce visual field neglect by forcing the client to look toward the side he doesn't favor. If you feel the visual field neglect cannot be altered (this is very hard to accomplish), simply arrange the pictures so they are always on his favorite side. If a client has a true visual field cut (the OT can help determine this if the M.D. hasn't already specified where the field cut is located), arrange the pictures appropriately.

- Here are some other ideas for the pictures. Enlarge them. Laminate them. Place velcro on the backs. Put the pictures on an upright board.

Activity: Place two pictures from the Core Vocabulary Pictures in front of the client. Name one and ask him to choose the correct one. Progress to four, six, and eight pictures if appropriate.

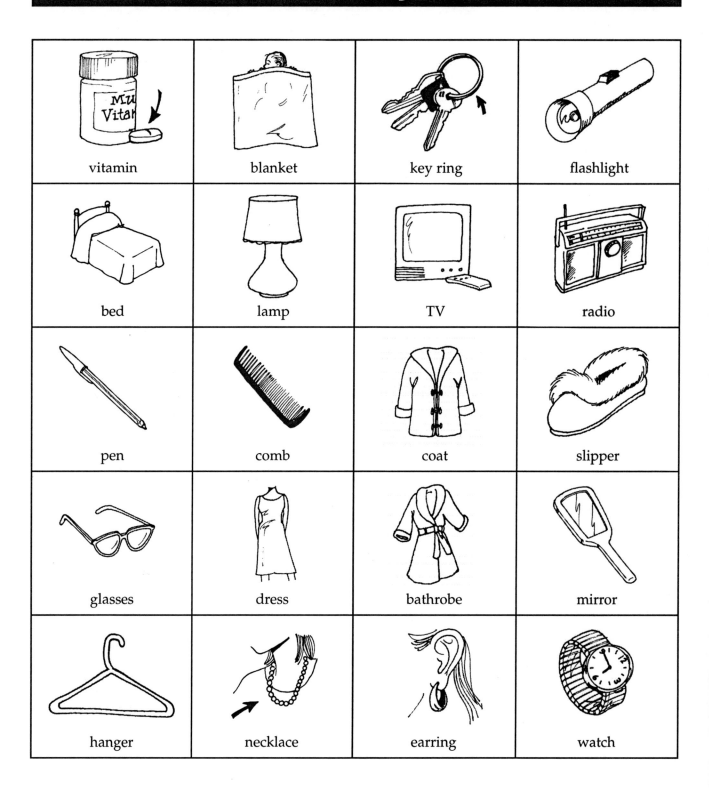

vitamin	blanket	key ring	flashlight
bed	lamp	TV	radio
pen	comb	coat	slipper
glasses	dress	bathrobe	mirror
hanger	necklace	earring	watch

Core Vocabulary Pictures

doctor	meal	drink	juice
magazine	napkin	dishcloth	spoon
cup	plate	hearing aid	knife
towel	toothbrush	lotion	clothing
shirt	shoe	sock	hat

Goal: The client will increase the ability to identify meaningful pictures at the appropriate visual field level on an AAC board 80% of the time.

Instructions: With the client's help, select a group of words from the Core Vocabulary Pictures on pages 22 and 23 that are meaningful to your client or based on his needs. Then construct an AAC (augmentative and alternative communication) board. Use inexpensive, lightweight plywood or stiff cardboard backing to make it. Glue, tape, or paste the pictures to the board in a configuration you want. Name a picture and ask the client to point to the correct one, or ask the client to name a picture and then have him point to the correct one.

Compensatory Strategies:
- Enlarge the pictures on a copier.

- Have the client use the board in various situations outside of therapy; for example, asking for medicine at the nurse's station, selecting a favorite food at dinner time, or participating in a group recreational activity.

- Vary the arrangement of the pictures on the board to compensate for visual field cuts or neglect. Cover the AAC board with clear contact paper or some type of lamination to protect it against damage.

- Use a one-inch silver ring to attach the board to the client's wheelchair, walker, or handbag to encourage more consistent use of the board.

- Reduce the size of the pictures so they can be carried in a wallet insert.

- Use a mouthstick or ask the OT for some tips to increase the client's physical abilities.

Activity: With the client's help, choose several pictures from the Core Vocabulary Pictures on pages 22 and 23. Photocopy them, cut them out, and arrange them on an AAC board. Name the pictures and ask the client to identify them.

(A note on AAC boards: High-tech AAC devices are sometimes quite expensive, and reimbursement for them is often difficult to obtain. Don't view a handmade AAC board as a therapy "failure." You are providing the client with a simple, functional communication system. With severely aphasic clients, this is sometimes the best you can do.)

Goal: The client will increase auditory comprehension to 90% accuracy for object word identification in gradually increasing visual fields.

Instructions: This activity is similar to the previous activity, Picture ID Using an AAC Board. The activity is for the client who can still read, but is so severely expressively aphasic, that an AAC word board is necessary. Use an AAC alphabet board if the client can still sequence letters to spell words. With the client's help, select a group of words meaningful to your client from the Vocabulary Word Lists on pages 26 and 27. There are 80 words—40 based on the Core Vocabulary Pictures and 40 additional words. Photocopy pages 26 and 27, cut apart into separate words, and place single words in front of the client. Ask him to identify the words as you name them. Following the instructions in the previous activity, construct or obtain an AAC board and attach the appropriate words. Name a word and ask the client to point to the correct one, or ask the client to name a word and then point to it.

Compensatory Strategies:

- Use an AAC notebook rather than a board for higher-level clients.

- Enlarge the words.

- Vary the arrangement of words on the board to compensate for visual field cuts or neglect.

- Use a one-inch silver ring to attach the board to the client's wheelchair, walker, or handbag to encourage more consistent use of the board.

- Reduce the size of the words so they can be carried in a wallet insert.

- Use a mouth stick or inexpensive head pointer if necessary. Ask the OT for some tips to increase physical abilities for your client.

- Have the client use the board in various situations outside of therapy; for example, asking for medicine at the nurse's station, selecting a favorite food at dinner time, or participating in a group recreational activity.

Activity: With the client's help, choose several words from the Vocabulary Word Lists on pages 26 and 27. Photocopy them, cut them apart, and arrange the words on an AAC board. Name the words and ask the client to identify them.

Vocabulary Word List

vitamin	blanket	key ring	flashlight	bed
lamp	TV	radio	pen	comb
coat	slipper	glasses	dress	bathrobe
mirror	hanger	necklace	earring	watch
doctor	meal	drink	juice	magazine
napkin	dishcloth	spoon	cup	plate
hearing aid	knife	towel	toothbrush	lotion
clothing	shirt	shoe	sock	hat

Vocabulary Word List

outside	telephone	frustrated	restaurant	pet
mad	perfume	aftershave	ambulance	breakfast
worried	computer	bedpan	roommate	dessert
soap	happy	sad	cologne	lunch
supper	pain	bowl	lip balm	friend
sign	dresser	door	window	dinner
walker	cane	inside	book	place mat
belt	pants	sweater	sheets	glove

The Source for Aphasia Therapy **27**

Goal: The client will increase the ability to understand common community signs to 90% accuracy.

Instructions: Photocopy the common community signs on pages 28 and 29. Cut them into sections and affix them to index cards if you wish. Laminate them or cover them with clear contact paper to protect them. Place 2-4 signs in front of the client. Name a sign and ask him to point to the correct one. Work your way up to four, ten, and twenty signs, if the client can name that many.

Compensatory Strategies:
- Enlarge the signs if necessary.
- Teach the client what the signs stand for, or name each sign before starting the activity.
- Make sure the client can clearly see the pictures.

Activity: Place pictures of the common signs in front of the client two at a time. Affix them to index cards if this is helpful. Name one and have him point to the correct one. Increase the visual field as appropriate.

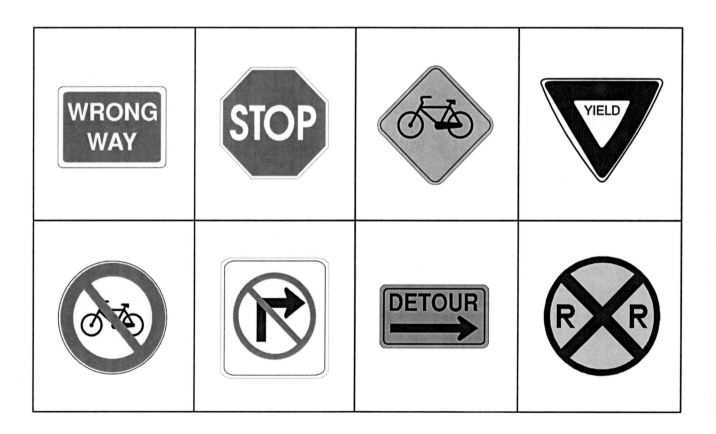

Goal: The client will increase auditory comprehension to 90% accuracy for simple yes/no questions.

Instructions: Ask the client the following simple yes/no questions. Explain that the questions will get more difficult as the activity progresses.

Compensatory Strategies:

• Repeat each yes/no question as often as necessary.

• Make the client feel comfortable. For example, make the questions conversational in tone. Preface a question with a little personal information. Show him the questions. Try to conceal your note-taking if you can.

• If the client thinks the questions are too simple or sound ridiculous, just convince him they'll get more difficult or agree with him. Do not condescend to the client.

Activity: Ask the client the following simple yes/no questions.

1. Is your name Bob/Mary?

2. Are you cold?

3. Have you eaten breakfast this morning?

4. Have you had lunch yet?

5. Are you too warm?

6. Is the light on in your room?

7. Is it raining outside?

8. Is it cold outside?

9. Have you gotten dressed yet today?

10. Did you have your hair cut today?

11. Have you taken your medicine today?

12. Is it daytime?

13. Is it dark outside?

14. Are you 65 years old?

15. Is this your home?

16. Is this your bedroom?

17. Have you seen your doctor today?

18. Have you seen your family today?

19. Are you married?

20. Do you have children?

21. Do you have grandchildren?

22. Are you retired from your job?

23. Do you live in an apartment?

24. Do you live in a condominium?

25. Do you live in a house?

26. Do you like to watch TV?

27. Do you like to read?

28. Did you have coffee with breakfast this morning?

29. Did you drink cranberry juice this morning?

30. Did you ever go to college?

31. Are you from Georgia?

32. Did you sleep well last night?

33. Are you 70 years old?

34. Do you have three children?

35. Do you have three grandchildren?

36. Do you wear bifocal glasses?

37. Do you wear trifocal glasses?

38. Do you wear dentures?

39. Do you wear a hearing aid?

40. Were you born in Florida?

41. Do you have any brothers and sisters?

42. Do you have two brothers?

43. Do you have a sister?

44. Do you have a sweater in your closet?

45. Is there a clock by your bed?

46. Is there a lamp on your nightstand?

47. Do you have any roommates here?

48. Do you have three roommates?

49. Do you think it will snow any time soon?

50. Do you have a TV in your room?

51. Do you like your therapy schedule?

52. Do you work best in the morning?

53. Do you get tired in the afternoon?

54. Do you usually take a nap every day?

55. Do you have a TV in your room?

Moderate Yes/No Questions

Goal: The client will increase auditory comprehension to 90% accuracy for moderate yes/no questions.

Instructions: Ask the client the following moderately complex yes/no questions. Explain that the questions will get more difficult as the activity progresses.

Compensatory Strategies:

- Repeat each yes/no question as often as necessary.

- Make the client feel comfortable. For example, make the questions conversational in tone. Preface a question with a little personal information. Show him the questions. Try to conceal your note-taking if you can.

- If the client thinks the questions are too simple or sound ridiculous, just convince him they'll get more difficult or agree with him. Do not condescend to the client.

Activity: Ask the client the following moderately complex yes/no questions.

1. Are you in a hospital right now?

2. Are you at your home right now?

3. Is this building a nursing home/center?

4. Are we in Dallas, Texas right now?

5. Is the current month February?

6. Is today Monday?

7. Is it the afternoon right now?

8. Is the current year 1997?

9. Is it summer right now?

10. Have you been here for five days?

11. Is today the 15th of the month?

12. Will tomorrow be Wednesday?

13. Will you be going home this week?

14. Did you watch the news on TV this morning?

15. Did you listen to the news on the radio this morning?

16. Was yesterday Sunday?

17. Did you call anyone on the telephone today?

18. Have you received any mail today?

19. Did the nurse give you a shot today?

20. Do you take medicine at every meal?

21. Do you have pain in your arm?

22. Have you been sick for about a week?

23. Will you be leaving the building today?

24. Do you have a doctor's appointment this week?

25. Have you ever broken a bone?

26. Have you ever been in a car accident?

27. Do you still drive a car?

28. Do you think you will be able to drive when you leave here?

29. Do you manage all of your own finances now?

30. Will you be able to manage your finances when you leave here?

31. Do you purchase all of your medicine at a small drug store?

32. Do you use a pillbox to organize your medications?

33. Are you taking more than five different medications?

34. Have you always done a lot of yard work?

35. Will you be able to do yard work when you leave here?

36. Does someone help you with yard work?

37. Do you have family members that live nearby?

38. Do you have a security system in your home?

39. Does your home have four bedrooms?

40. Does your home have three bathrooms?

41. Is there a library in your community?

42. Is the library near your home?

43. Do you live on a dirt road?

44. Have you been married more than once?

45. Do you have three doors that lead in and out of your home?

46. Is there a closet in one of your bathrooms at home?

47. Is there a closet in your bathroom here?

48. Did you exercise on a regular basis before you became ill?

49. Would you normally eat a tossed salad at the end of a meal?

50. Are you the oldest child in your family?

51. Do you have any brothers or sisters who are older than you?

52. Are all of your brothers and sisters still living?

53. Were you ever in a branch of the armed services?

54. Were you ever in the Air Force?

55. Were you ever in the Navy?

Complex Yes/No Questions

Goal: The client will increase auditory comprehension to 90% accuracy for complex yes/no questions.

Instructions: Ask the client the following complex yes/no questions. Explain that the questions will get more difficult as the activity progresses.

Compensatory Strategies:
- Repeat each yes/no question as often as necessary.

- Make the client feel comfortable. For example, make the questions conversational in tone. Preface a question with a little personal information. Show him the questions. Try to conceal your note-taking if you can.

- If the client thinks the questions are too simple or sound ridiculous, just convince him they'll get more difficult or agree with him. Do not condescend to the client.

Activity: Ask the client the following complex yes/no questions.

1. Is an inch shorter than a foot?

2. Is a foot 16 inches long?

3. Is a yard two feet long?

4. Does Tuesday come before Monday?

5. Is Thursday between Sunday and Wednesday?

6. Does a VCR play records?

7. Is a skyscraper taller than a shanty?

8. Is the number 15 between 10 and 25?

9. Is a stick bigger than a branch?

10. Is a piece of wood harder than a piece of paper?

11. Is short hair longer than long hair?

12. Are parents born before their children?

13. If you have a temperature, are you sick?

14. Do high-heeled shoes make you shorter?

15. If you are frightened, are you scared?

16. Do you pay a down payment before you buy a house?

17. Are you wet before jumping in a swimming pool?

18. Do you dry off before you get out of the pool?

19. Will you pay more for a car if you finance it rather than paying cash?

20. Do most people pay the entire amount in cash when they buy a house?

21. If you are second in line, are you near the front of the line?

22. If you have a coupon, will you pay full price?

23. If you are happy, does that mean that you are not sad?

24. Does everyone always speak the truth?

25. If you are poor, do you have a lot of money?

26. Is it better to eat vegetables rather than lots of sweets?

27. Will you be very healthy if you never exercise?

28. Do vertical blinds run up and down?

29. If you were shortchanged, were you cheated?

30. Is a penny larger in size than a nickel?

31. Are oranges and onions vegetables?

32. Is a feather lighter than a dictionary?

33. Does an hour equal 60 seconds?

34. If today is Wednesday, was yesterday Tuesday?

35. Does Thanksgiving come before Valentine's Day?

The Source for Aphasia Therapy

36. Are Mary and Fred considered female names?

37. Is July a month in spring?

38. Does Valentine's Day occur in March?

39. Does Valentine's Day occur before Independence Day?

40. Does a Persian cat have longer fur than a bulldog?

41. If you are wealthy, do you only have a little money?

42. Can Chris be a female and a male name?

43. Is it wise to save for a college education?

44. Should you call the gas company if you smell natural gas in your house?

45. Is a fork rounder than a spoon?

46. Is a platter larger than a dinner plate?

47. Should you leave your wallet on the seat of a car parked at the mall?

48. Is a cellular telephone wireless?

49. Should you dry your hair with an electric hair dryer while you take a bath?

50. Is scarlet considered a light red?

51. Would a VCR play cassette tapes?

52. Is a skyscraper smaller than a two-story house?

53. If you live in a subdivision, do you live in an apartment?

54. Are children born before their grandchildren?

55. If you have a coupon, are you paying a discounted price?

Goal: The client will increase auditory comprehension to 90% accuracy for simple paragraphs.

Instructions: Read a paragraph to the client. Ask him to answer the questions that follow. There are six questions—three context questions and three yes/no questions. Some questions may be easier or more appropriate for the client's comprehension level, so choose accordingly. Explain that the activity gets harder as it progresses. Try not to let the client read the paragraph himself since this is mainly a receptive language activity.

Compensatory Strategies:
- Read the paragraphs expressively.

- Break up the paragraphs into sentences if necessary.

- Vocally emphasize key words.

- Repeat the paragraph until the client understands it.

- Choose questions that match the client's level of verbal output. For example, a client with limited verbal output can answer yes/no questions by nodding or shaking his head.

Activity: Read each paragraph and have the client answer the questions that follow.

1. John came home from work with a splitting headache. His temperature was 102° by the time he got home at 5:45 p.m. He was sure he had the flu.

   a. Who had a headache?

   b. What time did he get home?

   c. How high was his fever?

   d. Was the story about a woman?

   e. Was the man sick?

   f. Was his fever higher than 102°?

2. Beatrice's grandson is graduating from college soon. In fact, the commencement ceremony is at 10:00 Saturday morning.

   a. Who is graduating from college?

   b. On what day of the week is the ceremony planned?

   c. What time will the ceremony begin?

   d. Is Beatrice's grandson graduating from high school?

   e. Is the ceremony planned for Saturday?

   f. Is the ceremony planned for Sunday?

3. Misty has developed an interest in photography. Yesterday afternoon at the mall, she purchased a new 35 mm camera made by Nikon®.

   a. What is Misty's new interest?

   b. What type of camera did she purchase?

   c. Where did she purchase the camera?

   d. Is Misty interested in cinematography?

   e. Did she purchase a camera?

   f. Was the camera made by Canon®?

4. When Paco awoke, he could smell the breakfast his wife, Mary, was cooking downstairs. He smelled coffee, bacon, and the irresistible aroma of homemade cinnamon rolls.

   a. What drink did Paco smell when he woke up?

   b. What is the name of Paco's wife?

   c. Name at least two foods Paco is having for breakfast.

   d. Could Paco smell lunch?

   e. Did Paco smell blueberry muffins?

   f. Was the woman's name Mary?

5. Betty was about to enjoy a full week of vacation away from her stressful job. On her first day of vacation, she walked into the kitchen to discover a large puddle of water seeping from under her refrigerator.

   a. How long would Betty be on vacation?

   b. On what day of her vacation did she discover the water?

   c. Where was the water leaking from?

   d. Did Betty discover the water on the second day of her vacation?

   e. Was water leaking from under her dishwasher?

   f. Did the leak happen on the second day of her vacation?

6. Marta's first grandchild was due any day now. She just got a call and discovered that her new grandson had been born last evening at midnight, weighing 8 pounds and 7 ounces.

   a. What was the grandmother's name?

   b. How much did the baby weigh?

   c. What time was the baby born?

   d. Was the baby born at noon?

   e. Was the child a boy?

   f. Was Marta's second grandchild about to arrive?

7. Juan had been experiencing problems with his car for the last two weeks. The mechanic informed him that his vehicle's computer would no longer work and the repair job would cost $1,000.

   a. How long had Juan been having trouble with his car?

   b. What had stopped working on his car?

   c. How much would the repairs cost?

   d. Had Juan experienced problems with his car for two weeks?

   e. Did Juan have problems with the manifold in his car?

   f. Did the repair job cost more than $500?

8. Steve likes to comparison shop for the best gasoline prices. The gas station in Fulton always has gas ten cents cheaper than any station in Brookfield.

   a. What did Steve comparison shop for?

   b. How much lower was the price of gasoline at the Fulton Street station?

   c. What cities were mentioned in the paragraph?

   d. Did Steve comparison shop for motor oil?

   e. Was something wrong with the computer in Steve's car?

   f. Was Brookfield's gas more expensive than Fulton's?

9. For the first time in franchise history, Bob's hometown professional baseball team has made it to the World Series. The last game of the series is scheduled for Saturday night at 8:00 at Yankee Stadium.

   a. What sport is mentioned in the paragraph?

   b. What time will the last game of the series begin?

   c. Where will the game be played?

   d. Is the paragraph about baseball?

   e. Is the last game scheduled for Friday night?

   f. Will the game be played at Tiger Stadium?

10. It had rained all night long. When Rita woke up at dawn and walked into her living room, she found a large puddle of water that had been caused by a leak in the roof near her bay window.

    a. What was the weather like?

    b. At what time of day did Rita enter her living room?

    c. What did Rita find in her living room?

    d. Had it been snowing all night?

    e. Did Rita enter her living room in the afternoon?

    f. Did Rita find the leak near her bay window?

11. Ishmael's dog was 12 years old and had been quite sick over the last year. At a veterinarian visit on Wednesday, Ishmael and the doctor decided to give the dog a new medication to ease his arthritis.

    a. What type of pet does Ishmael have?

    b. How old is the dog?

    c. What type of illness does the dog have?

    d. Is Ishmael's pet a dog?

    e. Is the dog 12 years old?

    f. Did they visit the vet on Tuesday?

12. When Harold received his telephone bill for $150, he knew something was wrong. Someone else had used his telephone number to make several expensive long distance calls to Mexico City.

    a. How much is the telephone bill?

    b. What is the man's name?

    c. To what city had the long distance telephone calls been made?

    d. Is the man's name Harold?

    e. Is his telephone bill $155?

    f. Were the calls made to Kansas City?

13. Bertha's home needed major repairs. The roof was 32 years old, the paint was peeling, and there was termite damage near her front door.

    a. How old was the roof on the house?

    b. What was the woman's name?

    c. Where was the termite damage?

    d. Was the roof 30 years old?

    e. Was the woman's name Bertha?

    f. Was the termite damage near the back door?

Simple Paragraphs, *continued*

receptive language

14. Raul wanted to surprise his wife on their 50th wedding anniversary. She would be so pleased when she saw the new red sedan he had parked in the garage.

    a. How long had Raul been married?

    b. What did Raul buy to surprise his wife?

    c. What color was the car?

    d. Had Raul been married for 60 years?

    e. Did Raul buy a new car?

    f. Was the car a sedan?

15. Martha decided to bake a German chocolate cake from scratch. She had all the ingredients on hand in her cabinet except for the sugar and chocolate.

    a. What was the woman's name?

    b. What was she planning to make?

    c. Name one ingredient that she did not have in her cabinet.

    d. Was the woman named Martha?

    e. Was she making a red velvet cake?

    f. Did Martha already have the chocolate in her cabinet?

16. The food served in the cafeteria of Richard's retirement community was terrible. Richard collected signatures on a petition to hold a community meeting for discussion of the matter.

    a. What was wrong with the cafeteria?

    b. Where was the cafeteria located?

    c. What did Richard do to help solve the problem?

    d. Was the food in the cafeteria very good?

    e. Was the cafeteria part of a large chain of restaurants?

    f. Did Richard collect signatures on a petition?

17. July was an extremely dry month. There was only a brief shower late in the month, and rainfall was six inches below normal for the year.

    a. What month was mentioned in the paragraph?

    b. How many showers occurred in July?

    c. How many inches below normal was the rainfall?

    d. Did the paragraph mention July?

    e. Was there more than one rain shower in July?

    f. Was the rainfall six inches below normal?

18. Mia was ready to buy a new home. She was certain that she needed three bedrooms, two bathrooms, and a large kitchen.

    a. What did Mia want to buy?

    b. How many bedrooms did she want?

    c. How many bathrooms did she want?

    d. Was Mia buying a new car?

    e. Did Mia want two bathrooms?

    f. Did Mia want three bedrooms?

19. Eugene needed a part-time job because he felt retirement was just too boring. He applied for a job at a local department store and was hired to work in the furniture department.

    a. Why did Eugene need a part-time job?

    b. Where did he apply for a job?

    c. What department was he hired to work in?

    d. Was Eugene retired?

    e. Did he apply for a job at a hardware store?

    f. Did Eugene end up working for the department store?

20. Charles had a special evening planned for Valentine's Day. He hired a limo to pick up his wife from work to meet him for a special dinner and then a Broadway show.

    a. What special occasion was mentioned in the paragraph?

    b. What type of vehicle was mentioned?

    c. Where were Charles and his wife going after dinner?

    d. Was the special occasion a wedding anniversary?

    e. Would they be riding in a limo?

    f. Would they have dinner after the show?

21. When Doris opened up the Homerville Public Library that morning, there was clearly something wrong. Someone had broken into the building, stolen several computers and some petty cash, and vandalized most of the bookshelves.

    a. What city is the library in?

    b. What had been stolen?

    c. What had been vandalized?

    d. Was the public library in Homerville?

    e. Had any computers been stolen?

    f. Were any of the bookshelves vandalized?

22. Ian and Mary had not been out to see a movie in four years. When they finally went to one, they were shocked to discover that a ticket now costs $6.50, and that a soft drink costs $3.00.

    a. How long had it been since the couple last saw movie?

    b. How much did a movie ticket cost?

    c. How much did a soft drink cost?

    d. Had it been five years since the couple saw a movie?

    e. Did a movie ticket cost $5.50?

    f. Did the soft drink cost $3.00?

23. John rented a movie from the video store on Friday. He didn't remember to return the video until Wednesday and he had to pay a $6.00 late fee.

    a. On what day did John rent the movie?

    b. On what day did John return the movie?

    c. How much was the late-return fee?

    d. Did John rent the movie on a Wednesday?

    e. Did John return the video on a Friday?

    f. Did he have to pay a $16.00 late-return fee?

24. Julio decided to pursue an advanced college degree at the age of 55. He planned to get his Master's Degree and Ph.D. in Psychology so he could become a licensed psychologist.

    a. How old was Julio when he went back to college?

    b. Name one degree he hoped to obtain.

    c. What field did he want to study?

    d. Was Julio in his forties?

    e. Did Julio want to obtain a Bachelor's Degree?

    f. Did Julio plan to study physical therapy?

25. Sarah is beginning her first day of volunteer work at the local hospital. She plans to work in the hospital gift shop from 9-6 every Wednesday.

    a. What is the woman's name?

    b. Where does she do her volunteer work?

    c. On what day of the week does she work?

    d. Is Sarah getting paid for her work?

    e. Is Sarah working from 9-6 p.m.?

    f. Is Sarah working on Wednesdays?

26. Elvira is an expert quilter. She now has a new assignment to construct a 100-square quilt to celebrate the 100th anniversary of the Women's Auxiliary Guild.

    a. What is Elvira an expert in?

    b. How many squares does Elvira need to make her quilt?

    c. What will the quilt be used to celebrate?

    d. Is Elvira an expert at quilting?

    e. Does she need 200 squares for her quilt?

    f. Is she making the quilt for a birthday celebration?

27. Lightning struck two TV sets in David's home last week. He was worried they couldn't be fixed, but the repairman had them ready within two days. The job cost $55.

    a. What happened to David's TV sets?

    b. How quickly did the repairman finish the job?

    c. How much did the TV repairman charge David?

    d. Were David's TV sets struck by lightning?

    e. Were his TV sets fixed within two days?

    f. Did the repairman charge David $50?

28. Charlotte enjoys interior decorating. So her daughter asked Charlotte to help select fabrics, furniture, and lamps for her new sun room.

    a. What does Charlotte enjoy doing?

    b. Name one thing Charlotte helped select.

    c. Which room did Charlotte help decorate?

    d. Does Charlotte enjoy decorating?

    e. Did Charlotte help her daughter select new things for the library?

    f. Did Charlotte help her daughter decorate a sun room?

29. Luc fell and broke his hip last week. Following surgery, he was scheduled for six weeks of physical therapy, three times a week.

   a. What happened to Luc?

   b. What type of treatment is he receiving?

   c. How often will he attend physical therapy?

   d. Did Luc break his leg?

   e. Did he have surgery?

   f. Did he receive occupational therapy?

30. Julia has suffered from dust allergies for most of her life. Her physician encouraged her to use special covers for her pillows and mattress and told her to replace the carpet in her home with hardwood or vinyl.

   a. What is the woman's name in the paragraph?

   b. What is Julia allergic to?

   c. What did her physician suggest?

   d. Is Julia allergic to household dust?

   e. Has she suffered from these allergies most of her life?

   f. Did the doctor suggest using a special spray on her carpet?

31. Lucia inherited a pair of diamond earrings from her grandmother. The jeweler who appraised the earrings told her they are two carats in weight and are worth approximately $4,000.

   a. What did Lucia inherit?

   b. Who gave Lucia the earrings?

   c. How many carats are in the diamonds?

   d. Did Lucia inherit a diamond ring?

   e. Did Lucia inherit the jewelry from her mother?

   f. Were the earrings worth more than $2,000?

32. Rosa walked into her dining room to find her two-year-old granddaughter holding a 100-year-old crystal vase. Rosa shocked the child into dropping the vase. It broke into a thousand pieces.

    a. What was the woman's name?

    b. How old was her granddaughter?

    c. How old was the crystal vase?

    d. Did Rosa have a two-year-old granddaughter?

    e. Was the crystal vase 80 years old?

    f. Did the crystal vase break?

33. Larry and Johann decided to go fishing early Saturday morning. They left at 5:00 a.m. and fished at Lake Sinclair until dark without catching a single fish.

    a. Who went fishing?

    b. On what day did they go fishing?

    c. On what lake did they fish?

    d. Did they leave at 6:00 a.m.?

    e. Did they fish on Sunday?

    f. Did they catch any bass?

34. It was time for Robert's 30,000-mile service tune-up on his truck. He took the truck to an independent mechanic who completed the tune-up and charged $300. The truck runs even better after the tune-up.

    a. How many miles were on Robert's truck?

    b. Where did Robert take the truck?

    c. How much did the mechanic charge?

    d. Was it time for the truck's 15,000-mile service tune-up?

    e. Did Robert take the truck to an independent mechanic?

    f. Did the mechanic charge $300?

35. Tara filed her federal income taxes this year and waited for her refund. With the electronic filing system, Tara received her $2500 refund in only five days.

    a. What kind of refund did Tara wait for?

    b. How long did it take for Tara to receive her refund?

    c. How much was Tara's refund?

    d. Did Tara use electronic income tax filing?

    e. Did Tara receive her refund in seven days?

    f. Did Tara receive a $2500 tax refund?

36. Ethel needed to use a cane to help her walk, but she didn't like the idea of using one. So her daughter painted the cane pink, green, and white and she attached some colorful ribbons to the cane. Now Ethel's happier.

    a. What did Ethel need to help her walk?

    b. What colors did Ethel's daughter paint the cane?

    c. What did Ethel's daughter attach to the cane?

    d. Did Ethel need a wheelchair?

    e. Did Ethel's daughter paint the cane red, white, and blue?

    f. Was Ethel happy after her daughter painted it?

37. Molly found her grandmother's pound cake recipe in the bottom of a drawer. She followed the recipe, entered the cake in a local contest, and won $75.

    a. Who created the recipe originally?

    b. Where did Molly find the recipe?

    c. How much money did Molly win?

    d. Was it Molly's recipe?

    e. Was it a recipe for pound cake?

    f. Did Molly win $100?

Goal: The client will increase auditory comprehension to 90% accuracy for moderately complex paragraphs.

Instructions: Read a paragraph to the client. Ask him to answer the questions that follow. There are eight questions—four context questions and four yes/no questions. Some questions may be easier or more appropriate for the client's comprehension level, so choose accordingly. Explain that the activity gets harder as it progresses. Try not to let the client read the paragraph himself since this is mainly a receptive language activity.

Compensatory Strategies:

- Read the paragraphs expressively.

- Break up the paragraphs into sentences if necessary.

- Vocally emphasize key words.

- Repeat the paragraph until the client understands it.

- Choose questions that match the client's level of verbal output. For example, a client with limited verbal output can answer yes/no questions by nodding or shaking his head.

Activity: Read each paragraph and have the client answer the questions that follow.

1. Daniel uses a cellular telephone in his sales job. His monthly bill is never less than $45. He decided to shop around and found a great deal with another company for $20 a month.

    a. What kind of phone does Daniel use?
    b. What kind of job does Daniel have?
    c. What was his monthly bill?
    d. What is the new rate?

    e. Is Daniel working in a sales job?
    f. Was his old cellular phone bill $45 a year?
    g. Does David use a cordless phone?
    h. Is his new cellular telephone rate more than $20 a month?

2. Juanita had always been interested in painting. She enrolled in a watercolor painting class at her local community college. The class met twice weekly for three months. By the end of the class, she could make beautiful paintings to decorate her living room walls.

   a. What was Juanita's interest?

   b. Where did Juanita take her art class?

   c. What type of painting did Juanita learn about?

   d. Where did Juanita hang her paintings?

   e. Was Juanita interested in pottery?

   f. Did she take an art class that was held in a gallery?

   g. Did the class meet three times a week?

   h. Did Juanita hang her paintings in her living room?

3. Martha got the flu in February even though she received her flu shot the previous October. She had a fever of 100° and had to miss three days of work. The doctor assured her that her bout with the flu would have been even worse without the flu shot.

   a. When did Martha get her flu shot?

   b. When did she come down with the flu?

   c. How high was her fever?

   d. How many days of work did Martha miss?

   e. Did Martha get smallpox?

   f. Did Martha come down with the flu in October?

   g. Did Martha get her flu shot in February?

   h. Did Martha miss three days of work?

4. Hassan loves working in his vegetable garden. His tomato plants produce juicy, red tomatoes until the first frost each fall. He sells the tomatoes for 50¢ each at a roadside stand.

   a. What is the man's name?

   b. What does he grow?

   c. When do his tomato plants stop producing fruit?

   d. How much does Hassan charge per tomato?

   e. Is the man's name Yassir?

   f. Does Hassan charge 60¢ a tomato?

   g. Do his tomato plants produce until late-summer?

   h. Does Hassan charge people by the bushel?

5. Jesse decided to participate in a research study designed to lower cholesterol. He signed up for the study at Emory University Hospital in Atlanta. Jesse followed a special diet and took medication that eventually lowered his cholesterol by 30 points.

   a. What did Jesse decide to do?

   b. Where did he participate in the research study?

   c. How much did he lower his cholesterol level by?

   d. What was the man's name in the paragraph?

   e. Did Jesse have high cholesterol?

   f. Did he participate in a research study?

   g. Was the study at Emory University?

   h. Did he lower his cholesterol during the study?

6. Bob and Terri's original home loan was for 30 years at 10% interest. Five years into the loan, they refinanced at 8 1/2% interest for 30 years. Two years later, they were able to refinance the loan for 15 years at 6 1/2% interest.

   a. What type of loan did Bob and Terri have?

   b. How much interest did they originally pay on their house?

   c. When they refinanced the first time, what was the interest rate?

   d. What was the interest rate when they refinanced the last time?

   e. Was their original loan written for 15% interest?

   f. Was their original loan written for 30 years?

   g. Did Bob and Terri refinance their loan three times?

   h. Did they end up with 6 1/2% interest for 15 years?

7. Each morning, Paul drank a cup of coffee before, during, and after breakfast. Before long, he began to feel nervous and jittery, and he started having trouble sleeping at night. When he changed to decaffeinated coffee, his problems went away.

   a. What does Paul drink every morning?

   b. How many cups of coffee does he drink every day?

   c. How did Paul begin to feel after he drank coffee?

   d. What did he have trouble doing at night?

   e. Did Paul have to change to decaffeinated coffee?

   f. Did Paul drink four cups of coffee a day?

   g. Does Paul sleep soundly now?

   h. Did Paul's problems go away?

8. Valentine's Day fell on a Sunday this year. Beth and Erik decided to celebrate on Saturday, so they made dinner reservations at Gregory's restaurant for 8:00 p.m.

   a. What special occasion is mentioned in the paragraph?

   b. What day of the week does Valentine's Day fall on in the paragraph?

   c. When did Beth and Erik celebrate Valentine's Day?

   d. What time were their dinner reservations?

   e. Is the paragraph about an anniversary?

   f. Are Beth and Erik going to celebrate on Sunday?

   g. Did they make reservations at Gregory's restaurant?

   h. Are the reservations for 7:00 p.m.?

9. Elizabeth and her family had portraits taken at Hammond's Photography Studio over the weekend. She picked up the proofs on Monday afternoon and ordered one 8x10, four 5x7s, and 20 wallet-sized photographs.

   a. When were the pictures taken?

   b. When did she pick up the proofs?

   c. How many 5x7s did Elizabeth order?

   d. How many wallet-sized photographs did she order?

   e. Did Elizabeth use Henry's Photography Studio?

   f. Were the pictures taken during the week?

   g. Did Paula order one 8x10 photo?

   h. Did she order 20 wallet-sized photographs?

10. Virginia always shops at Terry's Market because of the monthly specials. On the last Wednesday of each month, Terry's has a one-day sale. Virginia tries to stock up on all of her monthly groceries then. This month, Terry's Market is selling ground beef for 99¢ a pound and selling two-for-one laundry detergent.

    a. What is the name of the grocery store?

    b. On what day do they run the monthly specials?

    c. How long does the sale last?

    d. How much is the ground beef this month?

    e. Is the store called Virginia's Market?

    f. Are they selling ground beef for 99¢ a pound?

    g. Do they run specials on Tuesdays?

    h. Does the sale last for more than one day?

11. Larry McLean needs surgery to replace his left knee. He injured the knee playing college football 30 years ago. The onset of arthritis has made the knee almost nonfunctional. Larry got three medical opinions and will get his knee replaced this summer.

    a. What type of surgery does Larry need?

    b. What sport did Larry play?

    c. How many medical opinions did Larry get?

    d. When will Larry have his surgery?

    e. Did Larry need a hip replacement?

    f. Did Larry play professional football?

    g. Did Larry get three medical opinions?

    h. Did Larry have arthritis?

12. It's time for spring cleaning at the Taylor house. Each spring, Marge Taylor gives each of her three children different jobs. This year, she told Amy to clean all the windows and blinds. Paul has to wax the hardwood floors. Jeff needs to reorganize and clean up the garage.

   a. What is the family's last name?

   b. What type of cleaning will they do?

   c. How many children are in the household?

   d. What was Jeff's job?

   e. Were they cleaning in the middle of winter?

   f. Will Amy clean the chimney?

   g. Are there three children in the Taylor household?

   h. Will Jeff reorganize and clean the garage?

13. Shirley needs only 15 hours of college credit to complete her degree in Middle-Grades Education. She is currently teaching with a provisional teaching certificate. She has decided to complete the 15 hours over the summer during her break from teaching.

   a. How many hours of college credit does Shirley need to get her degree?

   b. When does she plan to complete the college courses?

   c. What type of degree does Shirley want to complete?

   d. What kind of certificate is Shirley teaching with now?

   e. Is Shirley already teaching?

   f. Does she plan to complete the college courses in the summer?

   g. Was Shirley teaching high school?

   h. Did Shirley register for 16 hours of classes?

14. Louise and Geraldo decided to get a dog to celebrate their recent retirement. They researched different breeds and chose an Irish setter because a bigger dog needs to be walked more. They figured this would help keep them in shape during their retirement years.

    a. What did Louise and Geraldo decide to get?

    b. What big event are they celebrating?

    c. What type of dog did they choose?

    d. Why did they choose an Irish setter?

    e. Did they want a kitten?

    f. Did they decide to get an Irish setter?

    g. Do they hope the dog will help them exercise more?

    h. Is it a big dog?

15. Every Friday night, the Martins have a date. They started doing this shortly after their first child was born. They go to their favorite Italian restaurant, order a bottle of wine with the meal, and always end up talking for hours. The restaurant gave them a 20th anniversary party last Friday night when they arrived for their regular 8:00 p.m. reservation time.

    a. On what day of the week do the Martins have their date?

    b. What type of restaurant do they go to?

    c. How many years have they been married?

    d. What time do they usually have dinner when they go out?

    e. Do the Martins have their date on Saturday night?

    f. Do they always go to an Italian restaurant on Friday?

    g. Have they been married for 25 years?

    h. Do they usually arrive at the restaurant at 7:00 p.m.?

16. Koto decided to join a book club. On the last Friday of each month, the group meets at a club member's home to discuss the latest book. For October, the club has decided to read a biography of Martha Graham, who was a pioneer of contemporary dance in the United States.

   a. What type of club does Koto belong to?

   b. On what day of the month does the club always meet?

   c. What month was discussed in the paragraph?

   d. What type of book will they read in October?

   e. Is Koto a member of a book club?

   f. Does the club always meet on the last Friday of each month?

   g. Will they read a biography of Isadora Duncan?

   h. Was Martha Graham a pioneer in theater?

17. Jack and Allison needed a new washer and dryer, so they went to Taylor's and chose a nice set. But Taylor's couldn't deliver the set for ten days, so Jack and Allison bought their washer and dryer from Simmons Appliances, because Simmons could deliver the set the same day.

   a. What is the name of the man in the story?

   b. Where did they first want to buy the washer and dryer?

   c. Where did they finally decide to buy the washer and dryer?

   d. What is the name of the woman in the story?

   e. Did Jack and Allison need a new dishwasher?

   f. Did Taylor's promise to deliver the appliances in less than a week?

   g. Did they buy the washer and dryer from Taylor's?

   h. Did they buy the washer and dryer from Simmons Appliances?

18. Every September, Heloise begins to buy gifts for the winter holidays. This year she bought a set of skis for her son and a new bike for her daughter. The total for the two gifts was $450.

    a. When does Heloise begin to buy gifts for the winter holidays?

    b. What did she buy for her daughter this year?

    c. What did Heloise buy for her son?

    d. What was the total for the two gifts?

    e. Does Heloise begin to buy gifts every September?

    f. Did Heloise buy a bike for her daughter?

    g. Did she buy skis for her son?

    h. Was the total $400?

19. Chan didn't have the money for a new car, so he looked for a used one. Last week, he found a six-year old sedan with only 50,000 miles on the odometer. He bought it for $2,000. He was pleased with the good deal he found.

    a. What did Chan buy?

    b. How old was the used car?

    c. How much did he pay for the car?

    d. How many miles were on the odometer?

    e. Did Chan buy a truck?

    f. Did he buy a two-year-old car?

    g. Was the car a sedan?

    h. Was Chan happy about the deal?

20. When Dana turned 50 years old recently, her hair was a salt-and-pepper color. She decided to dye her hair back to its original black color. But when she dyed it, it looked like her head had been dipped in black shoe polish. Dana had to pay $100 to have her hair lightened.

    a. What color was Dana's hair originally?

    b. How old is she now?

    c. What color was her hair just before she dyed it?

    d. How much did Dana pay to have her hair lightened?

    e. Is Dana 45 years old?

    f. Did she have any gray hair?

    g. Is Dana's original hair color blond?

    h. Did she pay $100 to have her hair lightened?

21. When her mother had a stroke five years ago, Margaret had to dress her mother during rehabilitation. But she found it difficult to dress her because of the cumbersome buttons and awkward sleeves. So Margaret made her mother clothes that slipped on easily and had velcro fasteners. Soon she was taking orders for clothes from the patients at the center. Now she has her own line of slip-on, geriatric clothing selling in major department stores.

    a. What happened to Margaret's mother?

    b. How many years ago did the stroke occur?

    c. Why was it diffcult for Margaret to dress her mother?

    d. What type of fasteners did Margaret use on her mother's clothes?

    e. Did Margaret's mother have a stroke?

    f. Are Margaret's new clothes unpopular with other patients?

    g. Were the regular clothes easy to put on?

    h. Does Margaret have her own geriatric clothing line?

22. After having a baby, Adalais took a six-month maternity leave. After six months, she didn't want to go back to her work as an attorney full-time. So she hired a nanny so she could return to work part-time.

    a. How many children did Adalais have?

    b. How long was her maternity leave?

    c. What type of job does Adalais have?

    d. What kind of worker did she hire to watch her baby?

    e. Did Adalais enroll her baby at a day care center?

    f. Is Adalais an attorney?

    g. Did she spend six months on maternity leave?

    h. Did she return to work full-time?

23. On the morning of December 23, 1989, a big snowstorm hit and paralyzed much of the state of Vermont. For ten straight days, the temperature didn't rise above 20°. Major interstate highways were closed. Some drivers had to drive for 24 hours to reach relatives for holiday celebrations.

    a. What year did the snowstorm hit?

    b. What state was affected by the snowstorm?

    c. How many days straight was the temperature under 20°?

    d. How long did some drivers drive to reach relatives?

    e. Did the snowstorm occur in January, 1989?

    f. Was California affected by the snowstorm?

    g. Was the temperature below 20° for 20 straight days?

    h. Did it take some people a day to travel to see relatives?

24. When Walter decided to work as an independently-contracted physical therapist, he didn't know what to do about insurance and other benefits. Then he contacted the American Physical Therapy Association and learned that he could purchase benefits from them at low rates. He bought $100,000 in life insurance, short- and long-term disability plans, car insurance, and professional liability insurance. Now he just needs to set up an IRA account for retirement benefits.

   a. What is Walter's job?

   b. Whom does Walter work for now?

   c. How much life insurance did he buy?

   d. Name one other benefit that Walter purchased.

   e. Is Walter a speech therapist?

   f. Did Walter buy his benefits from the American Insurance Company?

   g. Did Walter buy cancer insurance?

   h. Did Walter set up an IRA account?

25. Donna was never very committed to wearing a seat belt. When her mother got in the passenger seat of Donna's new red Buick yesterday, she insisted Donna buckle her seat belt. Twenty minutes later, they got into a serious car accident that left them both with cuts, bruises, and some broken bones. The policeman told them that the injuries would have been fatal if they hadn't used seat belts.

   a. What was Donna never very committed to doing?

   b. Who rode with Donna in the car?

   c. What color is Donna's car?

   d. What happened to Donna and her mother?

   e. Did Donna sometimes forget to buckle her seat belt?

   f. Did Donna drive a Ford?

   g. Was Donna injured in the crash?

   h. Did Donna have her seat belt on when the accident happened?

Goal: The client will increase auditory comprehension to 90% accuracy for complex paragraphs.

Instructions: Read a paragraph to the client. Ask him to answer the questions that follow. There are ten questions—five context questions and five yes/no questions. Some questions may be easier or more appropriate for the client's comprehension level, so choose accordingly. Explain that the activity gets harder as it progresses. Try not to let the client read the paragraph himself since this is mainly a receptive language activity.

Compensatory Strategies:
- Read the paragraphs expressively. Vocally emphasize key words.

- Break up the paragraphs into sentences if necessary.

- Repeat the paragraph until the client understands it.

- Choose questions that match the client's level of verbal output. For example, a client with limited verbal output can answer yes/no questions by nodding or shaking his head.

Activity: Read each paragraph and have the client answer the questions that follow.

1. This was the hottest summer Ada had ever experienced. The temperature had climbed to over 90° for the last 20 days. Ada's husband, Harold, noticed that it had become more difficult to cool the second floor of their home. Harold asked his neighbor and the neighbor suggested Harold use a garden hose to clean out the coils of the air conditioner. Harold followed the suggestion and felt a difference in 24 hours. Within three days, the cooling ability of the air conditioner was back to normal.

    a. What was Harold's wife's name?

    b. What was Harold's problem?

    c. How high did the temperature get?

    d. Whom did Harold speak to about the problem?

    e. What did the neighbor suggest that Harold do?

    f. Was the wife named Alice?

    g. Did Harold call a repair person to fix the problem?

    h. Did the temperature climb above 100°?

    i. Did Harold use a garden hose to clean the coils?

    j. Was everything back to normal in two days?

2. Maria put a pie in the oven and set the timer for 45 minutes. The telephone rang, and Maria answered it. It was her friend, Louise, informing her that she had come down with a bad case of the flu. Louise told Maria that they would be forced to cancel their shopping plans for tomorrow. The conversation continued for 20 minutes.

   a. What was Maria baking?

   b. Who called Maria?

   c. What was wrong with Maria's friend?

   d. How long did the conversation last?

   e. Who was coming to visit Maria tomorrow to go shopping?

   f. Was Maria baking a cake?

   g. Did Maria receive a telephone call from someone named Louise?

   h. Did the two women decide to go shopping the next day?

   i. Did the conversation last for 15 minutes?

   j. Was Maria's sister coming to visit to go shopping?

3. Paul is graduating from college in December. His grandmother is unsure about what to give him as a graduation present. She has consulted several different family members about it. Paul's grandfather suggested she buy a sweater. Paul's mother thought a book would be nice. Paul's sister felt he would like some new cycling shorts. In the end, Paul's grandmother decided to give her grandson some money for a skiing trip to Colorado he had planned for January.

   a. When will Paul graduate from college?

   b. Who suggested buying a sweater?

   c. Name another item that was suggested.

   d. What did Paul's grandmother decide to give him?

   e. Where will Paul go on his ski vacation?

   f. Will Paul graduate from college in June?

   g. Did Paul's grandfather suggest a sweater as a gift?

   h. Did someone suggest a new pair of pants as an appropriate gift?

   i. Did Paul's grandmother give him money as a gift?

   j. Is Paul going skiing in Utah?

4. It was 9:00 a.m., and for the third day in a row, Mr. Chin's morning paper was not on his doorstep. He waited another 30 minutes before he called the newspaper office. When the receptionist answered, Mr. Chin informed her that he hadn't received his newspaper for the last three days. She assured Mr. Chin that his paper would be delivered within the next two hours. She also gave him credit on his account for the missing papers.

   a. At what time did Mr. Chin suspect that his paper might not arrive?

   b. How long did he wait before he called the newspaper office?

   c. Whom did Mr. Chin speak with at the newspaper office?

   d. How many days did Mr. Chin not receive his newspaper?

   e. What did the receptionist do for Mr. Chin?

   f. Did Mr. Chin wait 45 minutes before calling the newspaper?

   g. Did Mr. Chin receive his paper yesterday?

   h. Was it 7:00 a.m. when Mr. Chin called the paper?

   i. Did Mr. Chin speak with an editor?

   j. Did Mr. Chin receive credit for the missing papers?

5. When Darlene got home, she sensed that something was wrong. She walked to the backyard to discover her dog, Buck, lying on the ground near the pasture fence. He had been badly injured. Darlene suspected that one of the horses must have kicked him. She bundled up Buck in a large quilt and put him in her truck. In 15 minutes, they arrived at the veterinarian's office. Buck had suffered lacerations that required stitches and three broken ribs. Four weeks later, his health had improved and he was as feisty as ever.

   a. What was the dog's name?

   b. Where did Darlene find Buck when they got home?

   c. What animal probably injured the dog?

   d. How long did it take to get Buck to the vet?

   e. What did Darlene use to bundle up Buck?

   f. Was Darlene's dog named Fido?

   g. Did the ride to the vet take 30 minutes?

   h. Did Buck lose an eye?

   i. Did Darlene think Buck was injured by a wolf?

   j. Were Buck's injuries fatal?

6. Kara ran several errands on Saturday morning to get ready for her brother's surprise birthday party later that night. She dropped by the drug store to pick up film for her camera. Then she picked up the cake at the bakery at 11:00 a.m. In the afternoon, Kara cooked various appetizers and finished cleaning the house. She expected 15 guests at 7:00 p.m. Her brother would arrive at 8:00 p.m. expecting to help Kara with her tax return. What a surprise!

   a. What time is the party supposed to start?

   b. What time did she pick up the cake?

   c. How many guests are attending the party?

   d. What did Kara cook in the afternoon?

   e. What will Kara's brother expect when he arrives?

   f. Was the party planned for the afternoon?

   g. Did Kara pick up the cake at 11:00 a.m?

   h. Will there be 10 guests at the party?

   i. Will Kara bake a cake?

   j. Did Kara tell her brother about the party?

7. Sofia has decided to rent a room at the local community center for her parents' 50th wedding anniversary. She's invited nearly 200 people from their small town for an open-house reception. The event is planned for June 25th from 2:00 p.m. until 6:00 p.m. Her sister, Elena, will handle all of the invitations. Her brother, Marco, will find the pianist. Sofia will take care of the catering. Sofia's daughter will order all of the flowers.

   a. Where will the party be held?

   b. What type of party is it?

   c. How many people are coming?

   d. What date is the party?

   e. What will Marco do?

   f. Will the party be at the banquet hall?

   g. Is Marco dealing with entertainment?

   h. Is the party planned for November?

   i. Will Sofia order all of the flowers?

   j. Will the party start at 6:15 p.m.?

8. José is starting a new job this Monday. Today is Saturday, and he has quite a few things to do before then. He needs to buy two new suits. He needs to go to an office supply store and buy a new daily planner and several ballpoint pens. On Sunday, he'll drive the twenty-mile commute to decide how much time he needs to get to work each day.

   a. When will José start his new job?

   b. How many new suits will he buy?

   c. What will José buy at the office supply store?

   d. How many miles will he drive to work?

   e. What will José do on Sunday?

   f. Will José start his new job Tuesday?

   g. Will he buy four new suits?

   h. Will he buy paper at the office supply store?

   i. Does José live ten miles from his new job?

   j. Will he take the bus to work?

9. After years of writing books in her field, Lisa decided to write a novel. The book will be historical fiction. Lisa's husband has a degree in history and has collaborated with her to complete the necessary research. It took Lisa a little less than a year to complete the manuscript. When she was finished, the novel contained 22 chapters and 374 pages. The process of finding a literary agent to sell her work was very frustrating. Finally Lisa decided to submit her manuscript to various publishers without using a literary agent. She and her husband agreed they would try for one year to sell the manuscript before abandoning the idea.

   a. What type of degree does Lisa's husband have?

   b. How long did it take Lisa to write the book?

   c. How many chapters are in the book?

   d. What was Lisa looking for?

   e. Whom did Lisa submit her manuscript to?

   f. Did Lisa's husband have a degree in history?

   g. Did it take Lisa more than a year to write the book?

   h. Did Lisa look for a literary agent?

   i. Did Lisa give up when she couldn't find a literary agent?

   j. Did Lisa's book have 20 chapters?

10. At 2:00 a.m., Yuri heard a loud thud downstairs. He bolted up in his bed and turned on the lamp. He called 911 and whispered to the operator to send police. Yuri then grabbed a rope ladder he always kept in his upstairs bedroom. He used the ladder to escape from the house before the intruder discovered his presence. When the police arrived, the burglar had already escaped with a VCR and several expensive pieces of silverware.

    a. What time was it when Yuri heard the intruder?

    b. What did Yuri tell the operator?

    c. What did Yuri keep in his bedroom that helped him escape?

    d. Where was Yuri when he heard the intruder?

    e. Name one item the thief stole.

    f. Did Yuri hear the intruder at midnight?

    g. Was Yuri on the first floor of his house?

    h. Did the thief take Yuri's TV?

    i. Did the thief take Yuri's VCR?

    j. Did the burglar escape before the police arrived?

11. Tomas had experienced trouble sleeping for the last four months. He asked for advice from several friends. Each friend described a different home remedy. Janos told him to drink warm milk. Sabina told him to take an antihistamine. Henri said reading just before bed should help him fall asleep easily. None of the suggested remedies were successful. Tomas then consulted his doctor who told him to stop drinking caffeine and to begin a daily exercise program of walking. Now Tomas is sleeping well once again.

    a. What was Tomas's problem?

    b. Whom did he talk to first?

    c. What did Henri tell Tomas to do?

    d. What did Sabina tell Tomas to do?

    e. What did the doctor tell Tomas to do?

    f. Did Tomas ignore his doctor's advice?

    g. Did he talk to his friends first?

    h. Did Henri tell Tomas to drink warm milk?

    i. Did Sabina tell Tomas to take an antihistamine?

    j. Does Tomas still have trouble sleeping?

12. Lara agreed to keep her granddaughter, Mary, for the next two weeks while Mary's parents took a trip to Japan. During the first week, Lara took Mary to the pool, to the park, and to a county fair. During the second week, Lara kept Mary busy with shopping trips, art projects, and a short computer course for children. Mary didn't have time to miss her parents!

    a. What was the grandmother's name?

    b. Where did Mary's parents go?

    c. Name an activity Mary did.

    d. How long were Mary's parents away?

    e. What didn't Mary have time for?

    f. Was the grandmother's name Lara?

    g. Did Mary's parents go to Jamaica?

    h. Did Lara take Mary to the movies?

    i. Were Mary's parents away for two weeks?

    j. Did Mary have time to miss her parents?

13. Mr. Gomez suffered a stroke three months ago which affected his ability to speak clearly. He was making good progress in his speech therapy, but his health insurance benefits only paid two months of therapy. His wife asked the insurance company to extend additional benefits to her husband. The company asked for letters from his doctor and speech pathologist explaining the medical need for more therapy. The doctor refused to write the letter. He doubted Mr. Gomez could make any more progress in therapy as this was the second stroke he had suffered. Mr. and Mrs. Gomez disagreed and looked for a new physician.

    a. What was Mr. Gomez's medical problem?

    b. How long did the insurance company pay for speech therapy?

    c. What did the insurance company want from the doctor?

    d. How many strokes has Mr. Gomez suffered?

    e. What did the Gomez family decide to do?

    f. Did Mr. Gomez suffer a heart attack?

    g. Did the doctor agree to write the letter to the insurance company?

    h. Was Mr. Gomez making progress in his speech therapy?

    i. Has Mr. Gomez suffered more than one stroke?

    j. Did the Gomez family keep the same doctor?

The Source for Aphasia Therapy

14. One Saturday night, a fierce storm swept through Savannah, Georgia. It began with severe thunderstorms bringing heavy rain. Then the rain turned into golf ball-sized hail. At 9:00 p.m., the weather service issued a tornado warning for the city. The weather forecaster predicted the tornado would enter the city around 10:00 p.m. Surprisingly, the tornado abruptly changed course and missed the city. Savannah sustained only some minor property damage due to trees felled by the storm. There were no serious injuries and no deaths.

   a. What night did the storm occur?

   b. When did the weather service issue the tornado warning?

   c. What did the tornado do?

   d. What caused minor property damage?

   e. How many people were seriously injured?

   f. Did the storm occur on a Sunday night?

   g. Did the weather service issue the warning at 9:00 p.m?

   h. Did the tornado touch down in Savannah?

   i. Was anyone killed in the storm?

   j. Was anyone seriously injured?

15. The big fair was this weekend. The fund-raising fair began at 10:00 a.m. on Saturday morning and continued until midnight. There were arts and crafts, carnival rides, and lots of food. The boys arrived at 11:00 a.m. and stayed until their parents picked them up just before supper. They enjoyed the jazz music much more than the pop music group. The Senator's speech was boring to the young boys. They spent most of the afternoon riding the Ferris wheel and the bumper cars.

   a. Where did the boys go?

   b. What time did the boys arrive?

   c. What time did the fair begin?

   d. What type of music did the boys prefer?

   e. Name a ride that the boys enjoyed.

   f. Did the boys go to a party?

   g. Did the boys leave after supper?

   h. Did the fair begin at 10:00 a.m.?

   i. Did the boys like the jazz music?

   j. Did the boys ride a merry-go-round?

16. Daniel felt he needed a change in his life. He had grown up in Detroit and had never lived in any other city. He researched other cities. He wrote to the Chambers of Commerce in three cities: Seattle, Atlanta, and Denver. In three weeks, he got packets from all three cities. After much debate, Daniel decided to move to Atlanta because of the warm climate.

    a. What was the man's name?

    b. Where did he grow up?

    c. Which cities did he write to?

    d. Where did he decide to live?

    e. Why did he choose Atlanta?

    f. Was the man's name Daniel?

    g. Was he living in Denver?

    h. Did he write to the Chamber of Congress?

    i. Did he decide to live in Detroit?

    j. Did he choose Atlanta because of the warm climate?

17. Mrs. Kirsch wanted every room in the house to receive a thorough cleaning this year. She devised a plan to clean one room each week. This would take 10 weeks to complete, but she felt it would be worth the time and effort. During the first few weeks, she and her husband cleaned only the three bathrooms. Then they moved to the three bedrooms. Next on her list was the kitchen. They totally reorganized the kitchen and had to spend two weeks on that room alone. Finally, they completed the den, living room, and dining room. After the cleaning project was complete, she and her husband took a cruise to the Bahamas.

    a. How many rooms did Mr. and Mrs. Kirsch clean each week?

    b. Which room did they begin with?

    c. Which room was totally reorganized?

    d. How many bedrooms are in the house?

    e. What was the total number of rooms the Kirsches cleaned?

    f. Did the Kirsches plan to clean two rooms each week?

    g. Did they begin their cleaning project with the bathrooms?

    h. Did they totally reorganize the living room?

    i. Did the Kirsches' home have three bedrooms?

    j. Did the Kirsches travel to Jamaica?

18. Mr. Taylor needed to buy a fax machine for his new home office. He talked to friends and researched several major brands. He had several specific requirements for his new fax machine. He needed a machine that could fax and copy documents as well as interface with his computer to become a printer. After searching for two weeks, he had narrowed the list to three machines. His final selection was based on price and performance records. Mr. Taylor was very pleased with the $350 machine that he purchased.

   a. What type of machine was Mr. Taylor looking for?

   b. Whom did Mr. Taylor talk to?

   c. Name one feature that was a requirement for the machine.

   d. How many weeks did Mr. Taylor search?

   e. How much did the fax machine cost?

   f. Was Mr. Taylor looking for a computer?

   g. Did Mr. Taylor talk to his boss about the purchase?

   h. Did Mr. Taylor expect his fax machine to copy?

   i. Did Mr. Taylor search for two weeks?

   j. Did the fax machine cost $350?

19. Kathy took Friday off from work to wait for the cable company to hook up her new television service. The technician was scheduled to arrive around 11:00 a.m. She waited until 1:00 p.m. and then called the cable office to check on the technician. The receptionist at the cable company told Kathy that the technician would arrive after 4:00 p.m. Kathy decided to go out for lunch. She returned at 3:30 p.m. to find a note on her door that the technician had already arrived to find no one home.

   a. What day did Kathy take off from work?

   b. What was the original appointment time?

   c. How long did Kathy wait before she called the cable company?

   d. Where did she go while she waited?

   e. What happened while she was gone?

   f. Did Kathy take Monday off from work?

   g. Was the technician originally supposed to arrive at 1:00 p.m.?

   h. Did Kathy wait two hours before she called the cable company?

   i. Did Kathy go shopping?

   j. Did the cable technician leave her a phone message?

20. Tara Lang has been a school teacher for 30 years and now she's retiring. During her first ten years, she taught fourth grade. After that, she spent five years teaching fifth grade. The final 15 years were spent with first-graders. Tara enjoyed that particular age group immensely. It was so rewarding to teach students how to read. In fact, the decision to retire has been a hard one. But the arrival of twin grandsons made her decision a little easier. Tara will move to Arizona as soon as the school year is over to be closer to her two new grandchildren.

    a. What was the woman's first name?

    b. Which grade did Tara teach for the first ten years?

    c. Which grade did Tara prefer teaching?

    d. What was the best thing about first grade?

    e. How many new grandchildren does Tara have?

    f. Was the woman's name Sara?

    g. Did Tara teach first grade for ten years?

    h. Did Tara prefer teaching second grade?

    i. Was teaching reading a favorite part of Tara's work?

    j. Will Tara be moving to Atlantis?

21. When Mr. and Mrs. Yeung arrived at the condominium in Ormond Beach, Florida, they were exhausted from the seven-hour drive. Their vacation condo had two large bedrooms and two baths upstairs. There was a half bath, a lovely living room/dining room combination, and a galley kitchen downstairs. The carpet was a beautiful sea green. The condo sat right on the beach. The Yeungs enjoyed the peaceful, secluded beach and had fourteen nights of restful slumber while listening to the ocean's constant waves.

    a. Where did the Yeungs go on vacation?

    b. Where did the Yeungs stay?

    c. How many bedrooms were in the condominium?

    d. What color was the carpet?

    e. How long was their vacation?

    f. Did the Yeungs visit Daytona Beach?

    g. Did the Yeungs stay in a hotel?

    h. Was the carpet ocean blue?

    i. Was there a living room downstairs?

    j. Was the beach secluded?

22. Construction will soon begin on the bypass highway around the city of McDonough. Ellen and her husband, Ron, own 10 acres of land right where the highway will run through. The city offered Ellen and Ron money for their house and property. Ellen had two more years before she planned to retire from her teaching position. She didn't want to sell. But Ron persuaded her to retire early and move to a house in Florida.

   a. What city did Ellen and Ron live in?

   b. How many more years did Ellen plan to teach?

   c. How many acres did they own?

   d. What was happening near their home?

   e. Where did they move?

   f. Did Ron and Ellen live in Dallas?

   g. Did Ron and Ellen own 20 acres of land?

   h. Did Ellen initially want to sell the house and land?

   i. Was Ellen planning to retire in five years?

   j. Did Ron and Ellen move to Florida?

23. Sally decided she needed a first-aid kit in her home. She went to a large, local drug store to find a preassembled kit. When she opened the kit, she felt many essential items were missing. Sally decided to compile the necessary items to make her own kit. She located a medium-sized plastic box with a handle. She bought Band-Aids®, hydrogen peroxide, bandages, ointment for burns and cuts, a small pair of scissors, a CPR mask, cotton balls, and salve for insect bites. Sally felt much more prepared with her new kit. She planned to take it with her on a camping trip next weekend.

   a. What was the woman's name in the paragraph?

   b. Where did Sally buy the preassembled first-aid kit?

   c. Name one item that was included in the kit Sally made herself.

   d. Where is Sally going next weekend?

   e. What was wrong with the preassembled first-aid kit?

   f. Was the woman's name Sandy?

   g. Did Sally go to the grocery store to buy a preassembled first-aid kit?

   h. Did Sally put rubbing alcohol in the first-aid kit she made herself?

   i. Did Sally place bandages in her first-aid kit?

   j. Is Sally going camping next weekend?

24. Ben and Cherie wanted to rent a movie for Saturday evening. Ben was determined to rent an action-adventure movie. Cherie preferred a comedy. The couple spent 45 minutes in the video store trying to make their decision. Finally, they made a compromise. They discovered if they rented a romantic drama for $5, they could receive two additional movie rentals for free. Ben and Cherie watched the romantic drama on Saturday night. On Sunday afternoon, Cherie watched her comedy while Ben worked in the garden. On Sunday evening, Ben watched his action-adventure while Cherie went to visit a friend.

   a. Who wanted to see the comedy?

   b. How long did they stay in the video store?

   c. How much did the video rental cost?

   d. What did the couple receive free of charge?

   e. What did Ben do while Cherie watched the comedy?

   f. Did Cherie want to see the comedy?

   g. Did they stay in the video store for an hour?

   h. Did the video rental cost $4?

   i. Did the couple receive two more movies free of charge?

   j. Did Cherie play golf while Ben watched the action-adventure?

25. Oscar knew he had to quit smoking. After suffering a heart attack, his doctor vehemently urged him to stop. Oscar tried to quit smoking by chewing nicotine gum. It didn't work. Then he used a nicotine patch and quit smoking for three months. He started again, though. Six months after becoming a smoker again, Oscar went to a seminar and was hypnotized to stop his smoking addiction. He also listened to audiotapes designed to curb his craving for cigarettes. Eating peppermint candy also decreased his desire to smoke. He finally quit.

   a. What health problem did Oscar experience?

   b. What method did he try *first* to stop smoking?

   c. What did he do at the seminar?

   d. What did he eat that helped to decrease his desire to smoke?

   e. Who urged Oscar to quit smoking?

   f. Did Oscar have lung cancer?

   g. Did Oscar try hypnotism first?

   h. Did Oscar listen to audiotapes?

   i. Did Oscar eat chocolate candy?

   j. Did Oscar's doctor urge him to stop smoking?

Reading Comprehension

Many aphasic clients will experience a disturbance in reading comprehension. In other words, their language impairment extends from speaking into other forms of language-based communication. This can be quite debilitating for the client who enjoyed reading prior to a neurological insult. Whatever the client's level of literacy, a disturbance in reading comprehension can often keep a client from achieving a higher level of independence.

As a clinician, you might value literacy and have a love of reading and literature. Realize that many of your clients may not share this interest. Therefore, the reading exercises in this section are function-based with stimuli from everyday life.

Make an extra effort not to inadvertently cause the client to feel stupid or foolish when beginning instruction in reading. You may want to say, "I'm not really teaching you to read. I'm helping to tweak your memory into remembering how to read." Also discuss how common it is for an aphasic client to experience a disturbance in reading comprehension. Put his mind at ease and do not condescend.

The following tasks are written in a very hierarchical manner. We begin by reading single letters and end the section by reading paragraphs. Therefore, select your client's appropriate level of difficulty and work up until a plateau is reached or until this section is successfully completed. If you need to go back to relearn or sharpen certain weak spots, then do so until you've reached a level your client is comfortable with. Homework for your client may be a good way to increase rapid skill development.

Goal: The client will increase the ability to read and match upper- and lowercase letters to 90% accuracy in order to improve reading skills.

Instructions: The client will read the cue letter on the left, then find its match on the right.

Compensatory Strategies:
- Enlarge the stimulus letters on a photocopier if necessary.
- Give the client a long, white index card to use as a marker to help scan from line to line. Cut a hole in the index card to allow the client to see one letter at a time if this helps.
- Have the client trace each letter with his finger or a pen.

Activity: Ask the client to read the letter on the left and find its match on the right. The first two and a half pages contain uppercase letters, and the last two pages have lowercase letters.

B	D	B	H	S	V	O
Z	D	T	Z	R	W	M
C	L	I	M	X	C	F
Y	J	O	E	T	Z	Y
D	S	D	R	G	X	H
X	B	E	X	Q	V	W

E		C	A	F	E	J	K
W		W	Z	Y	N	M	U
F		X	T	L	E	F	O
V		P	V	R	H	I	Q
G		D	B	T	G	X	Q
U		U	F	D	V	M	N
H		O	W	V	M	R	H
T		R	T	Y	I	F	E
I		L	Y	O	A	I	U
S		B	R	T	M	S	F

J		U	A	E	J	K	T
R		K	R	P	B	M	N
K		R	S	M	F	W	K
Q		Q	O	U	V	B	J
L		U	T	J	N	M	L
P		P	B	R	K	F	C
M		X	Y	N	W	M	S
O		U	C	G	B	P	O
N		F	M	T	N	K	L
A		I	E	A	R	K	N

n		b	n	p	m	r	s
q		g	b	p	q	t	u
a		r	s	o	a	b	u
l		l	t	b	k	x	y
o		o	c	e	i	u	a
m		x	y	v	r	n	m
p		f	g	q	p	g	h
k		r	k	v	t	b	x
r		t	b	p	m	n	r
j		j	g	b	q	y	z

s		t	k	z	s	r	v
i		l	n	j	g	t	i
t		t	x	n	u	a	o
h		m	i	k	r	h	n
u		m	u	a	n	o	e
g		b	i	t	p	h	g
v		m	x	v	n	y	z
f		l	k	j	e	f	h
w		r	h	w	m	v	t
e		e	o	i	u	a	c

Goal: The client will increase the ability to listen and identify upper- and lowercase letters to 90% accuracy in order to increase reading skills.

Instructions: Read the client the cue letter on the left and ask him to read and identify the correct one on the right. Use a piece of paper to cover the cue letter. Otherwise, the client will simply be matching letters as in the previous activity.

Compensatory Strategies:
- Photocopy, cut, and paste each letter on an index card so a group of cards can be easily manipulated. Photocopy and enlarge the letters if necessary.

- Take into account visual field neglect or visual field cuts.

Activity: Read the cue letter on the left without showing it to the client. Ask the client to point to the correct letter in the row of six on the right. The first two and a half pages contain uppercase letters and the last three pages contain lowercase letters. Start each command with the words, "Show me the letter _____."

L		A	T	B	L	E	F
Z		S	C	E	Y	X	Z
A		V	A	M	G	N	O
B		V	K	R	E	B	P
Y		E	K	Y	R	O	U
R		R	Y	X	P	Q	B

C		P	G	O	C	I	U
D		O	Z	C	E	B	D
X		Y	X	T	K	S	H
E		T	I	E	B	F	L
W		H	K	Q	M	W	N
F		F	G	H	E	L	T
S		U	Q	R	H	S	G
V		V	W	M	N	U	A
G		U	B	C	O	G	Q
T		E	T	F	H	M	N

H	M	N	I	H	A	T

O	O	T	B	P	K	R

I	E	M	C	I	T	H

M	M	N	D	R	F	E

J	T	J	I	L	M	Q

N	N	Z	P	R	Y	Z

U	B	U	W	M	C	D

Q	F	M	S	Z	Q	Y

K	K	R	T	B	E	F

P	P	B	S	F	K	G

p		b	m	l	p	q	m
f		f	e	h	j	l	t
k		r	k	j	f	g	b
z		p	n	m	r	t	z
w		m	n	w	r	k	y
v		v	n	w	s	r	t
u		e	b	a	u	t	r
g		l	d	g	p	j	b
d		o	p	z	y	m	d
h		n	h	t	x	v	w

j		j	q	p	g	s	i

o		m	w	o	a	e	u

i		y	j	l	k	i	z

t		r	m	v	j	t	i

r		q	r	b	e	h	n

e		e	o	c	i	u	a

x		v	x	w	z	y	k

d		g	f	k	t	d	b

y		n	m	u	y	o	a

m		q	v	b	n	c	m

b		b	d	g	q	p	m
n		t	v	s	r	m	n
q		p	q	g	h	t	i
s		c	u	o	t	s	r
x		v	w	x	r	t	z
l		t	l	h	k	b	d
y		j	w	y	p	g	b
c		i	a	g	o	c	e
z		z	s	t	r	y	m
a		p	a	d	k	g	h

Word Matching with Pictures

Goal: The client will increase the ability to read and match single words with picture cues to 90% accuracy in order to improve reading skills.

Instructions: Show the client the cue word on the left and have him read it aloud. Then ask him to match the cue word to one of the four words on the right. Tell the client to rely on the words first, then the pictures if it helps.

Compensatory Strategies:
- Enlarge and laminate the words and/or pictures for clearer and larger cues.

- Cut out the words and paste them on index cards. Let the client manipulate the cards and allow him ample response time. If you cut and paste the words/pictures, you can make many combinations.

- Tell the client not to become too dependent on the picture cues because they won't be used in the next activity.

Activity: Show the client the cue word on the left, let him read it aloud, and have him match it with the correct word on the right. Use picture cues if necessary.

1. comb	mirror	comb	toothbrush	lotion

2. lemons	cherry	watermelon	apple	lemons

The Source for Aphasia Therapy

3. **pizza**

soup	pizza	hamburger	sandwich

4. **giraffe**

fish	lion	giraffe	horse

5. **belt**

belt	pants	gloves	tie

6. **vest**

scarf	shirt	sweatshirt	vest

7. **backpack**	desk	locker	books	backpack

8. **vacuum**	blender	iron	toaster	vacuum

9. **knife**	fork	knife	chopsticks	spoon

10. **crib**	dresser	crib	bookcase	sofa

The Source for Aphasia Therapy

11. **glass**

| glass | cup | pan | plate |

12. **sleeping**

| smiling | sleeping | carrying | washing |

13. **dustpan**

| flashlight | broom | dustpan | mop |

14. **train**

| helicopter | ambulance | car | train |

The Source for Aphasia Therapy

Goal: The client will increase the ability to match single words to 90% accuracy in order to increase reading skills.

Instructions: Have the client read the cue word on the left aloud. Then ask him to match the cue word to one of the four words on the right. This is the same activity as the previous one, but without picture cues.

Compensatory Strategies:
- Write each word on an index card with a black marker so you can manipulate the cards easier.

- Point to each word if the client is having trouble. Continue to cue for increased visual skills and scanning.

- Don't read the words for the client unless he can't complete an item. You can sometimes give the client just the first sound of a word as a cue.

- Trace each letter in a word to aid the client's reading ability.

Activity: Have the client match the cue word on the left to the correct word on the right.

1. stop	wait	stop	go	caution
2. steak	fish	chicken	steak	fish
3. peach	pear	peach	apple	pineapple
4. beans	beans	peas	squash	corn
5. water	tea	juice	water	coffee
6. danger	exit	employee	danger	stop
7. women	men	child	baby	women

8. **petite**	small	medium	petite	large
9. **entrance**	entrance	exit	out	in
10. **poison**	plate	purple	poison	please
11. **shoes**	slippers	socks	sandals	shoes
12. **cut**	style	permanent	cut	blow
13. **wait**	stop	slow	fast	wait
14. **Jason**	Julie	Janice	Jason	Jay
15. **pet**	cat	dog	bird	pet
16. **stir**	stir	beat	fold	whip
17. **small**	large	small	medium	huge
18. **change**	dimes	nickels	change	coins
19. **elevator**	escalator	elevator	stairs	sidewalk
20. **closed**	closed	open	shut	closet

Goal: The client will increase the ability to identify/read and understand single words to 90% accuracy with picture cues in a visual field of four.

Instructions: Hiding the cue word on the left, read the cue word and ask the client to identify its match on the right. Have him point to the correct word and ask him to say it aloud. Tell him to rely first on the words, then on the pictures for help. Cover the picture cues so the client will have to rely on the words. Uncover them only if he needs help.

Compensatory Strategies:
- Take into account visual field neglect or visual field cuts.

- Mount the pictures on individual index cards so they can be easily manipulated on the table. Move the index cards into any formation that the client prefers for optimum visibility. To increase the difficulty of the activity, increase the visual field of pictures from four, to six, eight, or higher.

Activity: Hide the cue word on the left and the picture cues. Read the cue word on the left and ask the client to look at the four words on the right and find its match. Ask him to point to it and say the word aloud. Uncover the picture cues only if the client is having trouble identifying the cue word.

1. **banana**

| grapes | banana | strawberry | orange |

2. **blocks**

| Frisbee® | football | blocks | doll |

3. cereal

cereal	taco	pancakes	spaghetti

4. glue

ruler	computer	glue	chalk

5. dustpan

vacuum	broom	stool	dustpan

6. boots

earmuffs	sandals	boots	cap

7. **toaster**

fan	dishwasher	toaster	blender

8. **truck**

subway	truck	car	taxi

9. **bowls**

spoons	spatula	timer	bowls

10. **rake**

ax	rake	hoe	shovel

11. blender

| opener | microwave | refrigerator | blender |

12. stapler

| beater | hammer | stapler | gasoline |

13. pan

| plate | pan | wok | glass |

14. bicycle

| wagon | boat | stroller | bicycle |

Word ID without Pictures

Goal: The client will increase the ability to identify/read and understand single words to 90% accuracy in a visual field of four.

Instructions: Covering the cue word on the left, read the cue word aloud and ask the client to identify its match on the right. Tell him that in this activity, he will not have pictures to help him. Have him point to the correct answer and ask him to say it aloud.

Compensatory Strategies:
- Take into account visual field neglect or visual field cuts.
- The client should be fairly independent in his cueing by now.
- Mount the words on individual index cards so they can be easily manipulated on the table. Move the index cards into any formation that the client prefers for optimum visibility.

Activity: Hide the cue word on the left, read it aloud, and ask the client to find its match on the right. Tell him he won't have pictures to help him.

1. store	restaurant	store	library	pharmacy
2. jacket	dress	shorts	jacket	sweater
3. hat	belt	purse	tie	hat
4. slippers	pajamas	robe	gown	slippers
5. steak	steak	chicken	turkey	fish
6. clogs	sandals	tennis shoes	clogs	boots
7. ladies	ladies	gentlemen	boys	girls

8. **arm**	arm	leg	foot	head
9. **CD**	TV	radio	CD	video
10. **red**	black	red	white	blue
11. **van**	cab	bus	train	van
12. **news**	movie	news	game show	sitcom
13. **wash**	wash	dry	cut	style
14. **suitcase**	purse	bag	basket	suitcase
15. **bathroom**	kitchen	bedroom	dining room	bathroom
16. **bean**	fruit	vegetable	bean	steak
17. **husband**	husband	wife	sister	brother
18. **washcloth**	tissue	towel	washcloth	napkin
19. **stairs**	lounge	lobby	stairs	elevator
20. **plum**	peach	pear	pineapple	plum

Goal: The client will increase the ability to identify/read and comprehend two- to three-word phrases to 90% accuracy with picture cues.

Instructions: Ask the client to read aloud each cue phrase below. Then tell him to find its match from the four phrases below it. Ask him to point to the correct phrase.

Compensatory Strategies:
- Take into account visual field neglect or visual field cuts.

- Accommodate for poor visual skills by enlarging pictures, mounting phrases on index cards, etc.

- If you're using index cards, use a visual field of two to four to begin the task and gradually increase to eight if the client can handle it.

Activity: Have the client read each cue phrase and find its match from the four phrases below it. Use the pictures to help him find the match. Ask him to point to the correct answer.

---

1. **heavy coat**

fluffy sweatshirt   **wool sweater**   **silk dress**   **heavy coat**

---

2. **school books**

school books   **school newspaper**   **school yearbook**   **school workbook**

3. bowl of soup

slice of pizza	plate of spaghetti	three condiments	bowl of soup

4. square shape

square shape	rectangular shape	triangular shape	circular shape

5. bowl of cereal

stack of pancakes	bowl of cereal	club sandwich	hard-shelled taco

6. old wheelchair

soft chair	bicycle wheel	old wheelchair	cozy recliner

7. comic book

phone book	comic book	sheet music	garden magazine

8. ripe plum

Bartlett pear	Georgia peach	ripe plum	juicy apple

9. milk truck

milk truck	tow truck	moving truck	cement truck

10. pensive penguin

loud eagle	quiet duck	pensive penguin	proud pigeon

11. **two-dollar paper**

twenty-dollar sweater   **twelve-dollar pitcher**   **twenty-nine dollar toaster**   **two-dollar paper**

12. **two raccoons**

two kangaroos   **two raccoons**   **two rhinos**   **two horses**

13. **pink crayon**

green crayon   **pink crayon**   **blue crayon**   **purple crayon**

   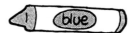 

14. **palm tree**

pine tree   **apple tree**   **tall grass**   **palm tree**

    The Source for Aphasia Therapy

Goal: The client will increase the ability to identify/read and understand two- to three-word phrases to 90% accuracy with picture cues.

Instructions: Have the client read the cue phrase aloud. Then ask him to look at the pictures below the cue phrase and point to the picture that matches the phrase he just read. Tell him there aren't words printed above the pictures as in the previous activity.

Compensatory Strategies:
- Use hand-over-hand assistance to guide the client if he seems very confused.

- Accommodate any visual difficulty to include decreased acuity, visual field neglect, visual field cuts, and/or decreased visual scanning.

- Allow the client to trace the cue words if this helps. Otherwise, reduce cueing, as you are heading towards the client's independence.

Activity: Show the cue phrase to the client and have him read it aloud. Then ask him to choose the picture that matches the cue phrase.

1. **shorter person**

2. **French dressing**

3. math book

4. soft pillow

5. two glasses

6. bowls of rice

7. **sliced cheese**

8. **cheese sandwich**

9. **soft blanket**

 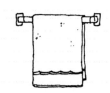 

10. **four polar bears**

11. **longest line**

—   —   —   —

---

12. **detour sign**

---

13. **largest circle**

     ◯   ◯   ◦

---

14. **bold, capital "G"**

g   g   **G**   G

Goal: The client will increase the ability to identify/read and understand simple sentences to 90% accuracy with picture cues.

Instructions: Hiding the cue sentence from the client's view, read the cue sentence to him. Ask him to point to the correct sentence from the two or four below it. Have him read it aloud. Hiding the cue sentence ensures that the client will not simply be matching the sentences, but reading and comprehending them. By this point in this series of activities, the cue sentences and answers are not enlarged and are not in bold type, but appear as they would in normal reading material.

Compensatory Strategies:
- Photocopy the pictures with their sentences and enlarge them to accommodate visual impairments before you begin this activity. Place the pictures in a configuration comfortable for the client.

Activity: Hide the cue sentence and read it aloud. Ask the client to point to the correct match out of the two or four choices and read the sentence aloud. Use the picture cues if necessary.

---

1. The top button is unbuttoned.

The top button is unbuttoned.   The bottom button is unbuttoned.

---

2. The monkey is in the tree.

The monkey is next to the tree.   The monkey is in the tree.

3. The bottom drawer is open.

The bottom drawer is open.

The top drawer is open.

4. The girl is sleeping in the top bunk.

The girl is sleeping in the top bunk.

The girl is sleeping in the bottom bunk.

5. The swimmer is near the pier.

The swimmer is far from the pier.

The swimmer is near the pier.

6. The dog ate the food.

The dog will eat the food.

The dog ate the food.

7. They are playing baseball.

   They are playing basketball.   They are playing baseball.

8. Let's go to the toy store.

   Let's go to the toy store.   Let's go to the hardware store.

9. There are two flowers.

   There are three flowers.   There are two flowers.

10. The shark is chasing the fish.

    The wolf is chasing the deer.   The shark is chasing the fish.

11. She is sliding.

She is singing.	She is sliding.	She is skating.	She is swinging.

12. It's a cloudy day.

It's a cloudy day.	It's a sunny day.	It's a rainy day.	It's a windy day.

13. Bread smells good.

Bread smells good.	Rolls smell good.	A rose smells good.	Pizza smells good.

14. It's snowing.

It's raining.	It's sunny.	It's windy.	It's snowing.
			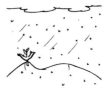

Goal: The client will increase the ability to identify/read and understand simple sentences to 90% accuracy without pictures cues.

Instructions: Tell the client you will show him four sentences. Tell him that you will read one of the sentences and he will point to the sentence you read. (There are no cue sentences in this activity, so choose whichever sentence of the four you wish.) After each identification trial, you can ask the client to read the sentences aloud as an extension activity. After you go through the activity, you can do it again varying your cue sentence.

Compensatory Strategies:
- Use a piece of paper to block out text that may distract the client.

- Encourage the client to point to the words as he reads/says them or allow him to trace letters with his finger. At this point, the client should be cueing as independently as possible. Allow ample response time.

- Don't give away the answer with your eyes as you read the cue sentence.

Activity: Choose a sentence among the four and read it aloud. Ask the client to identify the one you read.

---

1. Please go to the grocery store.

    Get butter and eggs today.

    Buy some orange juice, please.

    Orange juice is good for you.

---

2. Call the doctor after four o'clock.

    The man sold his car at six o'clock.

    I will be home at seven o'clock.

    It's ten o'clock now.

---

3. The roast will cook in two hours.

    My casserole cooked too long.

    Don't wait too long to cook the meat.

    The meat is overcooked.

4.   The robbery happened at the bank.   The news from the hospital is good.

      We saw it on the news.   The robbery survivor lived.

---

5.   I wrecked my car on Maple Drive.   The agent said the car was totalled.

      It's a nice car.   My insurance rate went up.

---

6.   I put $1000 in the bank.   The $1000 is a down payment.

      The bank will be closed Monday.   The bank makes money on ATMs.

---

7.   Please wash my car today.   We'll need soap and a hose.

      The car wax is in the laundry room.   The car seat is ripped.

---

8.   Please call a plumber.   The clog is in the sink.

      The drain is clogged.   The clog isn't in the tub.

---

9.   I need some new clothes.   I need a new shirt.

      I need some new pants.   I need some new boots.

    The Source for Aphasia Therapy   **115**

10.   It will be rainy on Friday.   Let's enjoy the sun Saturday.

       Friday is the last day to go.   It will rain on Sunday.

___

11.   Exercise will help keep you healthy.   John never gets off the couch.

       Louise exercises five times a week.   Sammy just talks about exercise.

___

12.   I've always wanted a van.   A small car might not be safe.

       An SUV is too big for the road.   My husband really wants a truck.

___

13.   I started a new diet yesterday.   Drinking water is good for me.

       I plan to stay in shape this year.   I lost fifteen pounds last month.

___

14.   Writing a book is my dream.   I will have to do a lot of research.

       I have taken some writing classes.   I may write a book about my trip.

___

15.   My sister went hiking in Canada.   I plan to go snow skiing this winter.

       The Rockies are in Canada.   We will visit Panama in August.

16.   We brought home a new puppy.   My daughter suggested a monkey.

          My wife prefers dogs to cats.   My favorite kind of dog is a setter.

---

17.   The party is planned for Saturday night.   Mary has planned all the food.

          Barry will take care of the drinks.   Alma has bought a gift already.

---

18.   I prefer to wait until it's on video.   John goes to the movies twice a week.

          They want to see the movie now.   Bob watches TV a lot.

---

19.   Football season is much too short.   I heard about the strike in the NBA.

          Baseball is very popular in Cuba.   My son made the swim team.

---

20.   Literature was my favorite subject.   I can't do math without a calculator.

          We can learn a lot from history.   I wish all schools would teach phonics.

---

21.   Cumbia is a kind of dance.   The band played all night.

          Dancers hit the floor in waves.   The bongo is a type of drum.

Question Comprehension

Goal: The client will increase reading comprehension to 90% accuracy for functional questions.

Instructions: In this activity, the client will read and answer sets of twenty questions that are divided into *What*, *Who(m)*, *Where*, *When*, and *How* questions. For each set, there are ten multiple choice and ten non-multiple choice questions. If his writing skills are good, he may write out the answers or circle the correct letters. If writing skills are not intact, he may verbally give the answer.

Compensatory Strategies:
• The client should now be self-cueing for skills such as visual scanning or visual neglect.

Activity: Have the client read the following questions aloud and answer them verbally or in written form.

What Questions

1. What name below is considered a boy's name?
   a. Paula
   b. Paul
   c. Patricia

2. What name below is considered a girl's name?
   a. Harriett
   b. Harry
   c. Henry

3. What time would you usually eat dinner?
   a. 6:00 a.m.
   b. 12:00 p.m.
   c. 6:00 p.m.

4. What job is considered the most dangerous?
   a. teacher
   b. firefighter
   c. doctor

5. What day comes right after Friday?
   a. Sunday
   b. Tuesday
   c. Saturday

6. What piece of furniture do you usually sit on?
   a. chair
   b. table
   c. china cabinet

7. What is the darkest color of these three?
   a. yellow
   b. black
   c. white

8. What color is traditionally worn at a funeral?
   a. black
   b. white
   c. pink

9. What food can be scrambled?
   a. tomatoes
   b. eggs
   c. steak

10. Which food is usually served hot?
    a. ice cream
    b. cheesecake
    c. spaghetti

11. What is your favorite color? _____

12. What is your middle name? _____

13. What is a job you have done for a living?_____

14. What grade did you finish in school? _____

15. What is your favorite season of the year?_____

16. What type of car do/did you drive? _____

17. What is your doctor's name? _____

18. What helps you to go to sleep at night? _____

19. What do you like to eat for breakfast? _____

20. What is your address? _____

Who(m) Questions

1. Who helps to keep an office building or school clean?
   a. principal
   b. secretary
   c. custodian

2. Who enforces laws?
   a. firefighter
   b. police officer
   c. tax commissioner

3. Who is the leader of a sports team?
   a. coach
   b. teacher
   c. trainer

4. Whom do you see when you have a toothache?
   a. doctor
   b. dentist
   c. nurse

5. Whom do you consult if your dog is sick?
   a. nurse
   b. pharmacist
   c. veterinarian

6. Who cleans houses?
   a. gardener
   b. housekeeper
   c. manicurist

7. Who would you see if you sued someone?
   a. attorney
   b. doctor
   c. paralegal

8. Who cooks food in a nice restaurant?
   a. hostess
   b. waiter
   c. chef

9. Who performs alterations on a bridal gown?
   a. artist
   b. seamstress
   c. clerk

10. Whom do you get a haircut from?
    a. manicurist
    b. hair stylist
    c. makeup artist

11. Who is the most important person in your life? _____

12. Who is the head of your country? _____

13. Who was your favorite teacher in school? _____

14. Who taught you how to ride a bike? _____

15. Who is/was your wife/husband? _____

16. Whom would you call if you were sick? _____

17. Whom would you call if your toilet overflowed? _____

    _____

18. Whom would you call if you smelled gas in your house?

    _____

19. Whom would you call if you thought an intruder was in your house?

    _____

20. Who takes your order in a restaurant? _____

Where Questions

1. Where do you go to borrow a book?
   a. book store
   b. library
   c. grocery store

2. Where do you get emergency medical care?
   a. school
   b. police station
   c. hospital emergency room

3. Where do you usually go to eat quickly?
   a. fast food restaurant
   b. Italian restaurant
   c. Mexican restaurant

4. Where can you visit a beach?
   a. Florida
   b. Kansas
   c. Oklahoma

5. Where do you go to get new eyeglasses?
   a. dentist
   b. hearing-aid dealer
   c. optometrist

6. Where is a safe place to take a walk?
   a. busy highway
   b. public park
   c. construction site

7. Where is the best place to put a litter box in your house?
   a. living room
   b. bathroom
   c. basement

8. Where do you see zebras?
   a. hospital
   b. zoo
   c. your backyard

9. Where would you go to see an art exhibit?
   a. museum
   b. department store
   c. courtroom

10. Where do you put water to make it solid?
    a. oven
    b. cabinet
    c. freezer

11. Where would you go to buy a wrench? _____

12. Where would you like to go on vacation? _____

13. Where is the weather usually very cold? _____

    _____

14. Where can you buy a diamond bracelet? _____

15. Where do you get a car loan? _____

16. Where would you like to go on your birthday? _____

    _____

17. Where should you keep poisonous chemicals? _____

    _____

18. Where can you get your prescriptions filled? _____

19. Where can you get a tan?_____

20. Where can you buy a book? _____

Why Questions

1. Why would you call 911?
   a. for a hangnail
   b. in an emergency
   c. as a joke

2. Why would you wear a coat?
   a. to keep warm
   b. to keep cool
   c. to keep walking

3. Why would you eat at home rather than at a restaurant?
   a. It's more expensive.
   b. It's cheaper.
   c. A chef will cook for you.

4. Why might you have trouble paying for a new car?
   a. too much money
   b. too little money
   c. too much attitude

5. Why might you become overweight?
   a. You eat a balanced diet.
   b. You eat a diet high in fat.
   c. You exercise all the time.

6. Why might people ask you to repeat yourself?
   a. They just want to bother you.
   b. They are angry.
   c. They can't hear you.

7. Why should you never drink and drive?
   a. It makes you a better driver.
   b. You could have a car crash and hurt yourself and others.
   c. You won't be able to hear.

8. Why should you always wear a seat belt when riding in a car?
   a. It can protect you in a crash.
   b. It looks nice.
   c. The car won't start without it.

9. Why is it good to watch the news?
   a. so you can take a nap in your chair
   b. to stay informed about current events
   c. to bother your spouse

10. Why should you brush your teeth at least twice a day?
    a. to keep your teeth and gums healthy
    b. to keep you from eating too much
    c. to keep you from getting a sore throat

11. Why does a cat have claws? _____

12. Why should you always be on time for meetings? _____

    _____

13. Why do people have arguments? _____

14. Why should you always keep your promises? _____

    _____

15. Why do some children need special education or remedial classes?

    _____

16. Why should you not smoke? _____

17. Why do cars have headlights? _____

18. Why do you need to study when you're in school? _____

    _____

19. Why do cats and dogs fight? _____

20. Why might you need to use a wheelchair? _____

How Questions

1. How do you find a telephone number you don't know?
   a. Call the operator.
   b. Look it up in a cookbook.
   c. Call the phone company.

2. How would you choose a good doctor?
   a. Ask a trusted friend.
   b. Look through the yellow pages.
   c. Ask an undependable friend.

3. How would you get your house painted if you were ill?
   a. Try to do it yourself, even though your health is not good.
   b. Ask some young kid to do it.
   c. Pay a painter to do a professional job.

4. How old must you be to legally drive in the U.S.?
   a. 16
   b. 19
   c. 21

5. How often should you brush your teeth?
   a. two times daily
   b. every other day
   c. once a week

6. How would you best remind yourself about an appointment?
   a. Just remember it.
   b. Tie a string around your finger.
   c. Keep a day planner notebook and write a reminder in the book.

7. How should you best obtain a new car loan?
   a. Go to the bank and fill out an application.
   b. Ask relatives to just give you the money.
   c. Ask a friend to loan you the money without interest.

8. How would you travel to London, England from the United States?
   a. by train
   b. by airplane
   c. by car

9. How would you stop payment on a check?
   a. Call the bank and pay a fee.
   b. Call the store and tell them not to take it to the bank.
   c. Call your accountant and ask him to take care of the problem.

10. How could you raise money for a local charity?
    a. Ask poverty-stricken citizens to give money.
    b. Ask large corporations to donate money.
    c. Ask children to donate their allowances.

11. How could you best organize weekly housekeeping chores?

    _____

12. How do you get your holiday shopping done? _____

    _____

13. How should you keep your body healthy? _____

    _____

14. How can you keep your flowers from dying during dry weather?

    _____

15. How could you raise money for a community project? _____

    _____

16. How would you find a pet to take home? _____

17. How can you learn to drive? _____

18. How do you find a job? _____

19. How often do you shop for clothes? _____

20. How can a person remain honest in a dishonest world? _____

    _____

Paragraph Comprehension

Goal: The client will increase the ability to read and understand paragraph-level material to 90% accuracy.

Instructions: Have the client read each paragraph and read the questions that follow. He should circle or point to the correct answer, or verbally give it.

Compensatory Strategies:
- Have the client use self-cueing strategies like tracing or sounding out.
- Keep your cueing to a minimum.
- Minimize external distractions.
- Let the client use a paper marker or other type of bookmark to keep his place and to cover distracting stimuli on the page.

Activity: Ask the client to read each paragraph and the questions that follow. He may circle or point to the correct answer or letter, or verbally give the answer.

1. Mae and Sam realized they were getting older when they started having trouble taking care of their yard. They decided to move into Friendship City, a retirement community of cluster homes. The organization does all yard work and all repairs on the houses through monthly association fees, which are $150 per couple.

What is this paragraph about?
a. the price of new homes
b. a decision about living arrangements for an elderly couple
c. a decision to retire

Where did Mae and Sam decide to live?
a. Coventry City
b. Friendship Village
c. Friendship City

Who will take care of the yard work in Mae's and Sam's new place?
a. the organization
b. family members
c. Sam

How much will the association fee be every month? _____

2. The baseball game was to begin at 5:00 p.m., but a thunderstorm started at 4:30. The game was delayed for two hours. It was midnight before Charles and Sarah finally got home. But they had stayed dry under the rain ponchos Sarah had insisted on bringing. Charles was glad he had listened to his wife.

What type of sporting event did Charles and Sarah attend?

a. basketball game
b. baseball game
c. football game

What time did the game start?

a. 5:00 p.m.
b. 4:30 p.m.
c. 7:00 p.m.

When did Charles and Sarah arrive home?

a. at noon
b. at midnight
c. They never made it home.

What did Sarah insist on bringing? _____

3. The Morrisses left for the beach at 9:00 a.m. and arrived on Tybee Island Beach an hour later. They spent all day playing with their three children. The oldest child, Brian, didn't put on enough sunscreen. He suffered a bad sunburn and missed two days of school.

Where did the Morrisses go?

a. the beach
b. a pool
c. a lake

Where was the beach?

a. Trouble Island
b. Treasure Island
c. Tybee Island

What is the oldest child's name?

a. Lisa
b. Bart
c. Brian

What happened to Brian? _____

4. Maria awoke Friday night at 2:00 a.m. with a terrible pain in her chest. She was sure she was having a heart attack. Her husband called 911. After two days in the hospital, Maria received an emergency gall bladder operation. Although she wasn't feeling well after the surgery, Maria was relieved that she had no heart problems.

Where did Maria feel pain?

a. in her leg
b. in her head
c. in her chest

When did Maria awake with the pain?

a. 2:00 p.m.
b. 2:00 a.m.
c. 2:00 f.m.

What did Maria's husband do?

a. called 911
b. freaked out
c. began throwing things at Mary

Why did Maria go to the hospital? _____

5. David underwent cancer surgery 16 days ago. Last night, he began feeling short of breath. He told his wife, Laura, and she looked up David's medications on the Internet. She told David that his medications might be causing the shortness of breath.

How long ago did David have surgery?

a. 60 days
b. 6 days
c. 16 days

Where did David's wife look for information?

a. a physician friend
b. the Internet
c. a neighbor

What did David feel when he was talking to his wife?

a. severe chest pain
b. shortness of breath
c. sore throat

What kind of surgery did David undergo? _____

6. When Amarita retired, she immediately bought a lake house on Lake Claire and put her old house up for sale. To her surprise, the house sold in only a month. Amarita invited her widowed sister to move into the lake house with her. It was nice to have a companion.

Who moved in with Amarita?

a. her friend
b. her daughter
c. her sister

How long did it take Amarita's house to sell?

a. one month
b. one day
c. one year

What was the name of the lake?

a. Lake Claire de Lune
b. Lake Sinclair
c. Lake Claire

Did Amarita's sister bring her husband to live with her at the lake? _____

7. Elizabeth was going through a mid-life crisis. She found it difficult turning 40. Her family was shocked when she announced she was changing professions. After being a nurse for 18 years, she decided to become a romance writer. She bought a black sports car, dyed her hair red, lost 30 pounds, and renewed her marriage vows after signing her first book contract.

What was Elizabeth experiencing?

a. a mid-life crisis
b. a death in the family
c. a torrid romance

How old was Elizabeth?

a. fourteen
b. forty
c. four

What was Elizabeth's first profession?

a. writer
b. teacher
c. nurse

What color did she dye her hair? _____

8. Sarah was shocked when her granddaughter was born weighing only 4 pounds, 11 ounces. Her daughter had taken excellent care of herself during the pregnancy, but did experience toxemia two weeks before delivery. But after two days of weight gain, mother and baby went home together. Sarah's granddaughter has turned out to be quite healthy. She is now eight years old and has just completed second grade.

What is the grandmother's name in this paragraph?

a. Sarah
b. Sandra
c. Sue

How much did the baby weigh at birth?

a. 4 pounds, 5 ounces
b. 4 pounds, 8 ounces
c. 4 pounds, 11 ounces

What illness did the mother have during the end of her pregnancy?

a. hives
b. toxemia
c. diabetes

How old is Sarah's granddaughter now?

a. seven
b. eight
c. eighteen

What grade did Sarah's granddaughter just finish? _____

Expressive Language

Expressive aphasia is very frustrating for the client who has experienced a neurological insult. It's difficult for us to imagine the host of emotions experienced by a client unable to make even basic needs and wants known to others. As speech-language pathologists, we witness this daily in rehabilitation units. Other therapists also become frustrated due to the breakdown in communication with the expressively aphasic client. It is our duty as therapists to provide a functional means of expressive communication for all clients.

This section gives you a step-by-step, hierarchical approach. Stimulus items are plentiful. Some of the more difficult tasks contain 100 stimulus items. Hopefully, this will relieve boredom when a certain skill must be practiced repeatedly.

Keep in mind as you use this book, that many clients will reach a plateau in therapy. If their neurological incident is more serious, or if this is a second, third, or even fourth neurological insult, some clients may never reach the conversational activities at the end of this section. Generally, if a client spends two to three weeks at a certain skill level and is unable to progress past this point in spite of extensive cueing efforts, then he has probably reached that plateau. Also keep in mind that it is the clinician's responsibility to devise external cueing strategies for caregivers and any self-cueing strategies that make expressive communication successful.

When a plateau in therapy has been reached, the clinician should then design a functional means of expressive communication for the client. This can be an AAC board or device, sign language, writing, or some other non-oral approach to verbal expression combined with any independent language skills that have been retained.

It is my hope that you will find the following activities to be engaging and functional. Enjoy your challenges ahead!

Automatic Sequences

Goal: The client will increase expressive language skills to within functional limits for producing automatic sequences.

Instructions: You'll have the client say common phrases, sentences, and songs along with you. Assure him that these automatic sequences are over-learned speech. In other words, let him know he won't be learning anything new, but retrieving simple language from the language part of his brain. It may be slow going at first, but once the activity gets going, most clients join in readily and are amazed at how simple it is for them to say these phrases and sentences.

Compensatory Strategies:
- Slightly over-exaggerate words and sounds. Provide a sing-song, rhythmic lilt to your voice.

- Hold up your fingers as you count with the client. Write down letters as you say the alphabet.

- Be positive. Tell the client he might feel a little silly at first, but that this activity is a good starting point for decreasing expressive aphasia.

Activity: Use these suggestions for automatic sequences:

➤ numbers by ones, tens, hundreds

➤ the alphabet

➤ vowels a, e, i, o, u

➤ client's address, phone number, name in a sentence

➤ nursery rhymes ("Jack and Jill," "Ole King Cole," etc.)

➤ familiar songs ("Happy Birthday," "Row Row Your Boat," etc.)

➤ popular songs ("National Anthem," "Somewhere Over the Rainbow," etc.)

➤ popular children's songs ("Three Blind Mice," "Jimmy Crack Corn," etc.)

➤ any song or list that the client is familiar with

Naming Objects within Sentences

Goal: The client will increase expressive language to 90% accuracy for naming common, functional objects (with cueing as needed).

Instructions: Collect 10-20 objects based on the Core Vocabulary Pictures on pages 22 and 23. Introduce an object to the client and ask him to identify it. Then read the client a sentence and hold up the object. Ask the client to name it when you get to the missing word.

Compensatory Strategies:
- Here are some additional cues. Say the first phoneme of each word. Write the first letter of the word (or the entire word) on a card and show it to the client. Say the sentence prompt while holding up the object, and mouth the target word silently as the client follows your lips.

Activity: Read each sentence to the client and hold up an object or picture of objects to help him complete the sentence. Accept any reasonable answer not listed.

1. I'll drink my coffee from this _____. (cup)

2. When my skin is dry, I'll apply some _____. (lotion)

3. I can write with a pencil or a _____. (pen)

4. My hands are dirty so give me that bar of _____. (soap)

5. I need to clean my hands, so lend me a _____. (washcloth)

6. I will dry off after a bath with a big, fluffy _____. (towel)

7. I bought a new pair of khaki _____. (pants)

8. He put on his pants and then his argyle _____. (socks)

9. I have a run in my _____. (pantyhose)

10. I need a new pair of tennis _____. (shoes)

11. My brother gave me a new button-down _____. (shirt)

12. To keep my teeth clean, I bought a new _____. (toothbrush)

13. I'll buy a new tube of _____. (toothpaste)

14. My vision is bad, so I need a new pair of _____. (glasses)

15. Get new batteries for my hearing _____. (aid)

16. To see my reflection, I'll have to use a _____. (mirror)

17. To go to the wedding, my wife will need a new _____. (dress)

18. I sleep with my head on a _____. (pillow)

19. It's cold, so I need an extra _____. (blanket)

20. I'm sick and it's time for me to take my _____. (medicine)

21. I read a good article in this week's _____. (magazine)

22. I brush my hair with a _____. (hairbrush)

23. To keep warm, I bought a new winter _____. (coat/sweater)

24. It's cold in the house, so I'll put on my _____. (sweater/slippers)

25. Before I go to bed, I put on my _____. (pajamas)

26. I'll cut this steak with a fork and a _____. (knife)

27. My lips are dry, so I'll need some _____. (lip balm)

28. You'll have to eat this soup with a _____. (spoon)

29. I want to write a note, so I need a piece of _____. (paper)

30. I just took off my wedding _____. (ring)

31. I tell time by looking at my _____. (watch/clock)

32. To wipe my mouth after eating, I'll need a _____. (napkin)

33. After brushing my teeth, I rinse my mouth with _____. (water)

34. I limp, so I need my walking _____. (cane, stick)

35. I'd like to read a good _____. (book)

36. Every day, I read the morning _____. (newspaper)

37. To shave, I will need a sharp _____. (razor)

38. If I want to shave, I'll need a new can of shaving _____. (cream)

39. I'll hang my coat on this _____. (hanger/hook)

40. After my shower, I put on my bath _____. (robe)

41. It's cold, so I'll wear a pair of long _____. (underwear)

42. I'm going to talk on the _____. (telephone)

43. I'm going to take a long, hot, bubble _____. (bath)

44. My food is served to me on a _____. (plate)

45. To eat the meat, I will need a knife and a _____. (fork)

46. To listen to that station, I'll turn on the _____. (radio)

47. It needs to be louder, so I'll turn up the _____. (volume/music)

48. To walk on the cold floor, I'll need my other _____. (slipper)

49. If I have a medical problem, I'll go see my _____. (doctor)

50. The doctor's assistant is called a _____. (nurse)

51. It's time to go to the football _____. (game)

52. The game will be played at a _____. (stadium)

53. The stands will be full of _____. (fans)

54. On their heads, the players will wear _____. (helmets)

55. We will drive to the game in our _____. (car/truck/van)

Naming Objects without Sentences

Goal: The client will increase expressive language to 90% accuracy for naming common, functional objects with reduced external cueing.

Instructions: As in the previous activity, collect as many objects as possible based on the Core Vocabulary Pictures on pages 22 and 23. Introduce an object and ask the client to identify it. Tell the client you will *not* give him sentence cues this time to help him.

Compensatory Strategies:
- Describe the object and verbally express its function. If this is not effective, attach a simple carrier sentence to lead the client, "This is a _____."

- Give the client the first or second phonemes of the target word, "This is a br_____." (brush)

- If necessary, use the carrier sentence and the initial phoneme, then mouth the rest of the word silently.

Activity: Use objects based on the Core Vocabulary Pictures or from the previous activity and ask the client to identify each item as you pull it from a bag, or other secluded place. Explain that he will *not* receive sentence cues.

Picture Naming

Goal: To increase expressive language to 90% accuracy for naming common, functional pictures with cueing as needed.

Instructions: Photocopy the Core Vocabulary Pictures on pages 22 and 23 and cut them apart (if you wish). Ask the client to name each picture as you show it to him. Tell him you'll provide appropriate cueing if he has difficulty.

Compensatory Strategies:
- Use plain pieces of white paper to cover up other pictures to eliminate distractions. Many clients become distracted when presented with a page filled with pictures.

- Tape the pictures individually onto index cards and rearrange them.

- Select no fewer than 20 pictures per session.

- If the client is having extreme difficulty, use sentence prompts before each named picture. Use the sentence prompts from page 138 (Naming Objects without Sentences), or make up your own.

- Here are some additional cues. Describe the pictured object and state its function. Gesture the object's function. Provide the first phoneme of the pictured object. Point to the word below the pictured object to serve as a written cue. Silently mouth the pictured word.

Activity: Introduce a picture from the Core Vocabulary Pictures to the client and have him name it.

Expressing Object Functions

Goal: The client will increase verbal expression to 90% accuracy for expressing object functions with single word and phrase responses.

Instructions: Select either pictures from the Core Vocabulary Pictures on pages 22 and 23, or objects *based* on the Core Vocabulary Pictures. Use at least 20 objects or pictures per session to better determine that accuracy levels are valid and reflect a large enough sample of responses. Ask the client to first name the object/picture, and then to tell you how each object is commonly used. For example, hold up a spoon and the client will say, "spoon." Then say, "Yes, this is a spoon. What do you use a spoon for?" Continue until all 20 object functions are stated.

Compensatory Strategies:
- Repeat this activity until the client reaches 80 to 90% accuracy.

- Give the client carrier phrases like, "This is a _____. It is used for _____."

- Give a gestural cue to help the client find the object's function; for example, sip soup with an imaginary (or actual) spoon.

- Give the first sound of the object's name. Mouth the words silently.

Activity: Present the client with pictures of objects from the Core Vocabulary Pictures or based on the Core Vocabulary Pictures, and have him name each object and then give the object's function.

Goal: The client will increase verbal expression to 90% accuracy for single-word responses during sentence completion tasks.

Instructions: Tell the client you will read a sentence and leave out the last word. He will verbally provide the missing word. Explain that the sentences are ones he's probably heard many times in his life. There are three sets of questions: simple, moderate, and complex. Answers are provided for the simple and moderate questions, but not the complex ones. The simple questions are fairly straightforward. The moderate questions may have more than one right response, so be flexible with the client. The complex questions are more open-ended and difficult. For the complex questions, try to reduce cueing.

Compensatory Strategies:
- Give the client the first phoneme of the answer. Use a carrier sentence and the initial phoneme, then mouth the rest of the word silently.

- If the client's expressive aphasia is more severe, you can rhythmically beat sounds of the sentence or write down the missing words on index cards.

- Allow the client to read the sentence along with you if he needs a visual cue.

- If the client is having extreme difficulty, it may be time to make an AAC board or communication book/wallet to augment the client's limited expressive language for basic needs and wants.

Activity: Read each sentence and have the client fill in the missing word. Provide compensatory cues as needed.

Simple Sentences

1. You can go up or _____. (down)

2. He's either tall or _____. (short)

3. You're either big or _____. (little, small)

4. She could be skinny or _____. (fat)

5. It's black or _____. (white)

6. It's wet or _____. (dry)

7. Go now or _____. (later, never)

8. Go right or _____. (left)

9. Come here or go over _____. (there)

10. Go in the summer or the _____. (winter, spring, autumn)

11. It's sunny or _____. (rainy)

12. I'm either young or _____. (old)

13. You're either happy or _____. (sad)

14. It's either expensive or _____. (cheap, inexpensive)

15. Go at night or during the _____. (day)

16. I'm always early or _____. (late)

17. We can go before or _____. (after)

18. You're either too hot or too _____. (cold)

19. Sometimes you go too fast or too _____. (slow)

20. Give me a lot or give me just a _____. (little)

21. He keeps going in and _____. (out)

22. That one is on top and the other one is on the _____. (bottom)

23. I will put it on or take it _____. (off)

24. Keep your hair long or cut it _____. (short)

25. Your hair is curly or _____. (straight)

26. It went from the ceiling to the _____. (floor)

27. The volume is either too high or too _____. (low)

28. My pants are either too loose or too _____. (tight)

29. The load could be heavy or _____. (light)

30. You can work in the daytime or at _____. (nighttime)

31. You can close the door or leave it _____. (open)

32. The traffic light tells you to stop or _____. (go)

33. It went from my head all the way down to my _____. (feet, toes)

34. Have something to eat or _____. (drink)

35. My eyes were either shut or wide _____. (open)

36. Did you tell me the truth or did you tell me a _____? (lie)

37. The dishes are either clean or _____. (dirty)

38. I stayed from the beginning till the _____. (end)

39. The mattress was either too hard or too _____. (soft)

40. You can work either days or _____. (nights)

41. It's raining cats and _____. (dogs)

42. I'm going to turn over a new _____. (leaf, page)

43. He was born with a silver spoon in his _____. (mouth)

44. It's time to go, so let's hit the _____. (road)

45. I'm tired, so let's call it a _____. (day)

46. I always play by the _____. (rules)

47. She can talk a blue _____. (streak)

48. The early bird gets the _____. (worm)

49. Early to bed, early to rise, makes a man healthy, wealthy, and _____. (wise)

50. Wake up and smell the _____. (coffee, roses)

51. The old neighborhood has gone to the _____. (dogs)

52. I want a house with a white picket _____. (fence)

53. Your granddaughter has been as good as _____. (gold)

54. He's watching me like a _____. (hawk)

55. I'm so hungry, I could eat a _____. (horse)

56. I need this piece of pie like I need a hole in the _____. (head)

57. A stitch in time saves _____. (nine)

58. You're as snug as a bug in a _____. (rug)

59. He's always the odd man _____. (out)

60. She's as slow as a _____. (turtle, snail)

61. He told us about a land of milk and _____. (honey)

62. He's as sharp as a _____. (tack)

63. It's as smooth as _____. (silk)

64. I laughed until I _____. (cried)

65. You need to shape up or ship _____. (out)

66. I don't care if you're the last person on _____. (earth)

67. I could take it or leave _____. (it)

68. I'm as blind as a _____. (bat)

69. She gave him a run for his _____. (money)

70. I read that book from cover to _____. (cover)

71. That man is as tough as _____. (nails)

72. All of this has made me sick to my _____. (stomach)

73. That was a bitter pill to _____. (swallow)

74. I'll just save it for a rainy _____. (day)

75. I'm going to shake things up around _____. (here)

76. Just take things one day at a _____. (time)

77. He's as strong as an _____. (ox)

78. Remember to stop, look, and _____. (listen)

79. You need to learn reading, writing, and _____. (arithmetic)

80. You're skating on thin _____. (ice)

81. She's as sweet as _____. (sugar)

82. That man is as straight as an _____. (arrow)

83. He slammed the door right in my _____. (face)

84. That woman has always been the talk of the _____. (town)

85. Now I have a roof over my _____. (head)

86. I caught the thief red- _____. (handed)

87. You are the light of my _____. (life)

88. You are the apple of my _____. (eye)

89. I'm going to shop until I _____. (drop)

90. I'm as mad as a _____. (hatter)

Moderate Sentences

1. It's noon, so it's time to eat my _____. (lunch)

2. I'm tired, so I'd like to take a _____. (nap)

3. I just woke up, and I need to brush my _____. (teeth, hair)

4. I'm thirsty, so I'd like a glass of _____. (water)

5. To write this note, I need a piece of paper and a _____. (pen/pencil)

6. I am 65 years _____. (old)

7. I feel sick, so please take me to the _____. (doctor, hospital)

8. Turn on the TV so I can watch the 6:00 _____. (news, show)

9. Let's go for a ride in the _____. (car)

10. Meet me for dinner at seven _____. (o'clock)

11. The pharmacist gave me these _____. (pills)

12. My hair is too long, and I need to get it _____. (cut, done)

13. I'm cold, so turn up the _____. (heat)

14. It's so hot that you should turn on the _____. (fan)

15. My drink is warm, so please put some ice in my _____. (glass)

16. It's time for us to leave and go back _____. (home)

17. I tell time by looking at my _____. (watch, clock)

18. The TV isn't loud enough, so please turn it _____. (up)

19. On my finger, I wear a wedding _____. (ring)

20. I need some adhesive for my false _____. (teeth)

21. Please get me some cream and sugar for my _____. (coffee)

22. It's time to put on my socks and _____. (shoes)

23. When I get out of the shower, I put on my _____. (bathrobe, clothes)

24. Please answer the telephone when it _____. (rings)

25. Please pass the salt and _____. (pepper)

26. I'm about to eat, so I need to go wash my _____. (hands, face)

27. Take a bath with soap and _____. (water)

28. I need to brush my teeth, but I need a tube of _____. (toothpaste)

29. To eat my meat, I need a fork and a _____. (knife)

30. To wipe my mouth, I need a _____. (napkin)

31. On my head, I wear a baseball _____. (cap, hat)

32. I can't see very well, so I need a new pair of _____. (glasses)

33. Please get me some new batteries for my hearing _____. (aid)

34. I have trouble walking up the _____. (stairs, hill)

35. I need to sit down in this _____. (chair)

36. To help me get to sleep, I drink a glass of warm _____. (milk)

37. These sandals are worn out, so I need a new pair of _____. (shoes)

38. I would like someone to polish my finger _____. (nails)

39. After a long drive, I need to use the _____. (bathroom)

40. It's dark in here, so please turn on the _____. (light)

41. We've finished dinner, so let's wash the _____. (dishes)

42. We're going to celebrate our 50th wedding _____. (anniversary)

43. I'd like to curl up on the couch and read a good _____. (book)

44. We've been on a trip, so check the answering _____. (machine)

45. Every hour, I hear the chiming of my grandfather _____. (clock)

46. The dog is scratching at the door to go out for a _____. (walk)

47. Someone should mop the kitchen _____. (floor)

48. We have so much junk that I plan to have a garage _____. (sale)

49. The doctor told me to open wide and stick out my _____. (tongue)

50. I was so excited that I felt like jumping up and _____. (down)

51. I want a hamburger, French fries, and a chocolate _____. (milk shake)

52. I can tell by the look on your _____. (face)

53. My head is full of wiry, gray _____. (hair)

54. For my car, I need a new set of radial _____. (tires)

55. It's a sunny Saturday, so you'd better mow the _____. (lawn/grass)

56. Please go answer the _____. (telephone, door)

57. I enjoy walking around the _____. (block, neighborhood)

58. Whom will you invite to my birthday _____? (party)

59. This is my brother and over there is my _____. (sister)

60. Here are pictures of my eight _____. (children/pets)

61. The dentist put a new filling in my _____. (tooth)

62. The ambulance took him to the _____. (hospital)

63. In an emergency, always call _____. (911)

64. Why didn't you call me on your cellular _____? (phone)

65. I take my coffee with _____. (cream/sugar)

66. My eyes are drooping because I'm feeling very _____. (sleepy, tired)

67. The parade is set for the 4th of _____. (July)

68. Let's go to the high school football _____. (game)

69. I cooked dinner, so you can wipe the _____. (counter, table)

70. My emotions always show on my _____. (face)

71. Come over here and take a good _____. (look)

72. She sent me a gift, so I'll write her a thank-you _____. (note, card)

73. Put the letter inside the _____. (envelope/mailbox)

74. It's been so long since I've ridden a bicycle built for _____. (two)

75. I need to put the money in my checking _____. (account)

76. Take my temperature to see if I have a _____. (fever)

77. Doctors will never make house _____. (calls)

78. They told me to sit out here in the waiting _____. (room)

79. I'm only five feet _____. (tall)

80. The bird is about to spread its wings and _____. (fly)

81. Hand me that belt so I can put it around my _____. (waist)

82. For Valentine's Day, he gave me a dozen red _____. (roses)

83. Every morning I read the _____. (newspaper)

84. Something in the grass is slithering like a _____. (snake)

85. Come have a piece of this strawberry _____. (cake, pie)

86. He sprinted across the four-lane _____. (highway)

87. When I fell, I sprained my _____. (ankle)

88. Could you please make me some macaroni and _____? (cheese)

89. I always love your chicken noodle _____. (soup)

90. I want to go sit down in the living _____. (room)

91. I'd like to hear you play the _____. (piano)

92. The elderly woman fell and broke her _____. (hip, leg)

93. For many years now, I've had to use a walking _____. (stick/cane)

94. I will be interviewing for a new _____. (job)

95. With this bad cold, all I do is blow my _____. (nose)

96. My son asked me to make a ham and cheese _____. (sandwich)

97. Let's listen to music on the CD _____. (player)

98. We got up on the dance floor and did the fox _____. (trot)

99. She was scared and shaking like a _____. (leaf)

100. I hope you're ready because it's time for us to _____. (leave, go)

Complex Sentences

1. It's time to go to the _____.

2. I need to tell you _____.

3. Come sit down in this _____.

4. I have to go wash my _____.

5. I forgot to take my _____.

6. I am writing with an ink _____.

7. My favorite color is _____.

8. My granddaughter has big, blue _____.

9. He was walking down the _____.

10. I heard the telephone because it was _____.

11. It's time for us to go _____.

12. I put the hat on my _____.

13. He placed the ring on my _____.

14. Pour me a cup of black _____.

15. Sign your name in black _____.

16. I bought a new pair of bedroom _____.

17. I haven't seen my old friend in the last five _____.

18. That dinner you made was simply _____.

19. Please go outside and water the _____.

20. It's time to eat, so please come over here to set the _____.

21. I've been talking on the _____.

22. I'm so dirty that I need to take a _____.

23. I'm sorry I didn't hear the doorbell _____.

24. We used to have fun down at the drive-in _____.

25. I'm not feeling very _____.

26. She always has a sour look on her _____.

27. He counted from one to _____.

28. I went to the post office to pick up a certified _____.

29. For our vacation, we decided to go to the _____.

30. I will drink a cup of hot _____.

31. He walked over there to shake his _____.

32. I need to check out a book from the public _____.

33. She charged it on my credit _____.

34. To make a phone call, you now need a quarter and a _____.

35. The bird flew out the _____.

36. The baby bird fell out of her _____.

37. The baby needs to have her diaper _____.

38. Let's sit down side by _____.

39. He threw the ball and it broke my _____.

40. Please give me an answer to my _____.

41. It was so hot I decided to take off my _____.

42. I don't enjoy talking on the _____.

43. I have been working only three days a _____.

44. Be careful because that knife is very _____.

45. I smelled something burning on the _____.

46. He will drive me by the _____.

47. She was the winner of the _____.

48. I'm so tired of eating _____.

49. I'm so sick of drinking _____.

50. Put those bills on the _____.

51. I'll have to go get some gasoline for the _____.

52. My glasses used to be bifocals and now they are _____.

53. I always part my hair on the _____.

54. In the spring, we always plant _____.

55. After the rain, it's nice to see a _____.

56. I have one brother and two _____.

57. He graduated from Lakeshore High _____.

58. I got married in the year 19_____.

59. If it's raining, we will need our _____.

60. During the baseball game, I saw a player steal second _____.

61. I need some artificial sweetener to put in my _____.

62. I thought I heard an intruder in the _____.

63. That TV is much too _____.

64. In the sky, I saw a bolt of _____.

65. I need a pair of scissors so I can cut this _____.

66. You should call the power company about last month's _____.

67. I need help buttoning up my _____.

68. I will retire when I am _____.

69. He decided to start up his own _____.

70. I have a grandson named _____.

71. My granddaughter's name is _____.

72. It's about time for us to buy a new _____.

73. We decided to go out for a _____.

74. I'm going to can and freeze some of those fresh _____.

75. Go put that away in the _____.

76. Because I'm cold, I'll go get my _____.

77. We're going out to dinner next _____.

78. Our vacation is planned for the month of _____.

79. Could you please change the _____?

80. I'm going to sit down here and eat this piece of _____.

81. I fell outside on the _____.

82. I have been working too hard over the past _____.

83. Next April, I will turn _____.

84. Give me another serving of that _____.

85. My favorite holiday is _____.

86. My sister gave me a new pair of _____.

87. He's planning to arrive at _____.

88. We waited outside in the _____.

89. I'm really tired of looking at the _____.

90. I saved my money and I put it in a _____.

91. It got hot so I took off my _____.

92. My new outfit is blue and _____.

93. Put the paint over there on the _____.

94. Please share some of that candy with _____.

95. He went to sleep over there on the _____.

96. You need more salt and pepper in the _____.

97. In the newspaper, I only read about _____.

98. I would like to drink some _____.

99. They went hiking over by the _____.

100. I was shocked to hear about his _____.

Naming to Description

Goal: The client will increase verbal expression and word retrieval to 90% accuracy for single-word responses during naming drills.

Instructions: Tell the client you will describe certain objects. Then have him tell you what the object is. Think of this as a good "warm-up" activity for many clients who suffer word-retrieval difficulties. There are two sections: Nouns and Verbs.

Compensatory Strategies:
- Phonemic, syllabic, and gestural cueing is still permissible. But keep in mind that if you use these kinds of cues, then the client's prognosis for independent verbal expression worsens.

Activity: Read the following descriptions and have the client give you the answers.

Nouns

1. It has a back, a seat, and four legs. You sit down in it. (chair)

2. It has a collar and sleeves. It is made out of fabric. You wear it. (shirt)

3. It is usually white and it may have lines on it. Its shape is rectangular. You write on it. (paper/notepad)

4. It has numbers and buttons. There is a cord and a receiver. It rings and you can talk on it. (telephone)

5. It is a liquid. We all need it to live. It is clear and you should drink eight glasses of it daily. (water)

6. This is made out of metal. It has a handle. One end is rounded. You use it to eat soup. (spoon)

7. It is an animal. It has whiskers and claws. It says, "meow." (cat)

8. You wear this when you sleep. This clothing usually has two pieces. (pajamas)

9. This has many pages and a hard or soft cover. You read it. (book)

10. This is something that has a frame. It is rectangular. It has a mattress and box springs. (bed)

11. It has a sole, a tongue, eyes, and laces. You wear it on your foot. (shoe)

12. It has windows, doors, and a steering wheel. There are four tires and it needs fuel to keep going. (car, vehicle)

13. It is a major appliance. It has various temperatures. It gets hot and cooks food. (stove, oven)

14. It has a handle and bristles. It is used to keep your teeth clean. (toothbrush)

15. It comes in a bar or liquid. It makes suds. You use it to wash your hands and clothes. (soap)

16. This is usually made out of leather. It has a buckle. It goes around your waist. It holds your pants up. (belt)

17. This has a handle on one end and a point on the other end. You open it up and use it on a rainy day. (umbrella)

18. This is made of soft paper. It comes on a roll. You find it in the bathroom. (toilet tissue)

19. This is a string. It is usually white. The string is often coated with wax. You use it to get food out from between your teeth. (dental floss)

20. It is a liquid. It usually comes in a mint flavor. You use it to rinse out your mouth. (mouthwash)

21. This is a machine that has a screen and a keyboard. You use it to log onto the Internet and communicate with others. (computer)

22. It has handles or straps. A woman carries this to hold her money and other small, personal items. (purse)

23. This is an animal that many people have as a pet. It has fur. It wears a collar and it barks. (dog)

24. This is a season. It is cold and it often snows in the north. (winter)

25. It is usually made of metal and/or plastic. It has two round handles and two sharp blades. You use it to cut paper. (scissors)

26. It is made out of paper. You lick it to close it. Most people place letters inside this and put an address and stamp on the outside of it. (envelope)

27. This is a vegetable that looks like a little tree. It is green. Many people steam it to cook it. It is supposed to fight cancer. (broccoli)

28. This is a hot drink. It is black in color. Many people drink it when they wake up in the morning. (coffee)

29. This is frozen water. You put it in a drink to keep it cold. (ice)

30. This is a vehicle that has a cab and a bed. Most people use this vehicle to haul things. (truck)

31. This usually comes in packs of 20. It is bad for your health. You light it and smoke it. (cigarette)

32. It is made of wax. It has a wick. You can light it and place it on the dinner table. (candle)

33. It is made of paper or cloth. You use it during a meal to wipe your mouth and hands. (napkin)

34. It is hard on the outside. It has a strap and buckle. It goes on your head when you are riding a bike or motorcycle. (helmet)

35. This is a fruit that has a peel on the outside. It also has a stem. It can be green, red, or yellow. Some people say if you eat one of these everyday, the doctor will stay away. (apple)

36. This is something many women put in their hair. It is usually done in a hair salon. It puts curl into straight hair. (permanent)

37. This comes in granules. It is white. Most people keep it in a shaker on the kitchen table. You use it to season food. It is a condiment. (salt)

38. This is a season. Leaves fall from the trees. The air begins to get cooler and people start wearing sweaters. (autumn)

39. This is outside by your front door. It has a button to push that causes it to ring. You use it to let the homeowner know someone has come to visit. (doorbell)

40. It goes on the bed. It is soft. Most people place this under their head while they are sleeping. (pillow)

41. This goes up into the air. It takes people from place to place. It has an engine. (airplane)

42. These help you see better. You wear them on your nose. Sometimes they are bifocals or trifocals. (eyeglasses)

43. This is an electronic device that many people own. You watch movies, the news, and other programs on this appliance. (TV)

44. This is a day of the week. It comes two days after Tuesday and two days before Saturday. (Thursday)

45. This is a room in your house. It has a sink, a tub, and a toilet. (bathroom)

46. This is a place to live. It is usually in a building with many other units. You have to pay rent to live there. (apartment)

47. This is a very common illness with no real cure. It causes sneezing, a runny nose, and sometimes a cough. (cold)

48. It comes to your home in an envelope. A company sends it to you. It tells you that you need to mail the company money. (bill)

49. It is in your home. It can go up and down. It has panes made of glass and a screen on the outside. (window)

50. This is used in the summer in your house. It blows out cool air to reduce the heat in your house. (air conditioner)

Verbs

1. This is something you should do three times a day. It is vital for your health. It provides all the necessary nutrients for you body. (eat)

2. This is something you should do throughout the day. It keeps your body from dehydrating. You need a cup or a glass to do this. (drink)

3. You do this for about 6-8 hours each night. It is accomplished when you lie down, cover up, and put your head on a pillow. (sleep)

4. Many people do this when they sleep. It is often annoying and a husband/wife may have trouble sleeping because of this noise. (snore)

5. You do this for exercise. It is very good for you. You can do it slowly. You can do it outside or on an indoor track. Some people even do it at a shopping mall when the weather outside is bad. You do it with your legs. (walk)

6. You do this for exercise. You can do this in sprints or in marathons. You may also do it to get away from someone. (run)

7. You do this when you're walking or standing and you lose your balance and are suddenly no longer on your feet. (fall)

8. You learn to do this in school. You need a book, magazine, or newpaper to do this. (read)

9. You use your fingers to do this. You push keys on a board to make letters on a computer screen or a piece of paper. (type)

10. Many speech therapists encourage patients to do this. When you do it, you communicate and relate to others around you. You move your lips and tongue and annunciate. (talk)

11. This is a gesture of affection. It is accomplished by wrapping your arms around another person. (hug)

12. You do this when you show affection. You press your lips against another person's lips. (kiss)

13. You use your ears to do this. You can enjoy beautiful music and other sounds around you. (hear/listen)

14. You do this when you use your voice in a very loud manner. You may call for a child to come into the house or you may be angry at someone. (yell)

15. This is something you do following a good performance. You do it when you like the performance. You move your hands against each other rapidly and repeatedly to produce sound. (clap)

16. You do this with your feet to move a bicycle forward. (pedal)

17. This is something we do each day to keep our bodies clean. (bathe, wash, shower)

18. You might do this if you are sick or suddenly frightened. You begin to feel woozy, dizzy, and then you slump to the floor. You are unconscious for a short time. (faint)

19. You do this when you get a cold. You may also do this frequently in the spring if you have hay fever. Air is forced through your nose. (sneeze)

20. This action often accompanies a cold. It can keep you up at night. You should cover your mouth when you do this. If you do this enough, you'll get a sore throat. (cough)

21. When you do this you can look at the world and enjoy its beauty. You use your eyes to do it. (see)

22. This is another word for preparing food. You use food, an oven, and kitchen utensils, to do it. (cook)

23. You do this with a telephone. You pick up the receiver and dial the telephone. (call)

24. Your nose lets you to do this. When you have a bad cold, it is hard to do this. (smell)

25. You do this in your house. You can use a broom, mop, vacuum cleaner, dust rags, and furniture polish. (clean)

26. You must put food in your mouth to do this. The buds on your tongue help you do it. (taste)

27. To do this, you must take a test and receive a license. You could have a wreck while doing this. You use a car or other vehicle. (drive)

28. You do this every day when you put on clothes like pants, shoes, a sweater, a dress, etc. (dress)

29. You do this when you eat. You need teeth to accomplish this. You move your jaw up and down and grind food with your teeth. (chew)

30. You do this with your fingers. It is tactile. You place your fingers against something. (touch)

31. This is something you do with a machine to the grass in your yard. You don't do it when it's snowing, though. (mow)

32. You do this in a store. You go into the store, browse around, select an item, and then pay the clerk. (shop)

33. Your doctor tells you to do this to stay healthy. It involves physical movement to increase your heart rate. (exercise)

34. You do this with a pen and a piece of paper. You pick up the pen and move it along the paper to form words and sentences. (write)

35. You need an appliance that gets very hot to do this. You plug in the appliance, place an article of clothing on a board, and move the appliance over the clothing to erase the wrinkles. (iron)

36. You do this using a broom. You take the broom and move it over the floor to rake up small pieces of dirt and trash. (sweep)

37. You do this when you are sleepy. You open your mouth very wide. It tells you that it is time to lie down and go to sleep. (yawn)

38. You need music to do this. You use your voice to draw out words that go with the music. Your voice and words follow the melody. (sing)

39. You do this when cleaning a floor. You use a device with a long, wooden handle on one end and cotton strings or a sponge on the other end. (mop)

40. You do this by using a pencil or pen and art paper. You make images, inspired by creativity and vision, on the paper with the pencil. (draw)

41. You do this in an airplane. You board the plane, it takes off, and you move through the air. (fly)

42. You do this when you are sick or nauseated. The food you ate hours ago comes up from your stomach and out of your mouth. (vomit)

43. This is similar to singing, but you keep your mouth closed and use your voice to produce a tune. (hum)

44. This might happen when you walk. Your feet get tangled, you almost trip and fall, but you regain your balance and stride in time. (stumble)

45. People who enjoy preparing sweets do this. They mix ingredients to make items like pies, cakes, and cookies. (bake)

46. You do this by holding a book or magazine and moving your eyes across the page. (read)

47. You do this in a boat on the water. You use a pole with a line attached. There is a hook at the end of the line. (fish)

48. You do this to the clothes you take out of the dryer. You put the clothes together in an orderly fashion so you can put them in drawers. (fold)

49. You do this with a needle and thread. If a button falls off your shirt, you use the needle to put it back on. (sew)

50. You do this with wool yarn and two long needles. You use the long needles to weave the yarn together to make things like sweaters and blankets. (knit)

Two-or-More-Word Responses

Goal: The client will increase verbal expression to 90% accuracy for producing two-or-more-word responses during sentence completions/tasks.

Instructions: Read the client the sentence and ask him to complete the sentence with *two or more* appropriate words. It's not important what his answer is, as long as it's more than one word. Begin to fade cueing but assure the client that you will continue to provide cueing if he needs it.

Compensatory Strategies:
- Give appropriate gestural cues.

- Use index cards with the sentences written on them.

- Some clients (especially if it is a second or third stroke) will plateau at this point. If the client appears to be unable to progress past this skill level, you might set up an AAC system to augment limited verbal expression.

Activity: Read the client each sentence and have him fill in the completion with a phrase of two words or more.

1. I want to _____.

2. They had a _____.

3. Yesterday we went to _____.

4. Let's have some _____.

5. My daughter said to _____.

6. I have a son that _____.

7. We have something to _____.

8. Every spring, I _____.

9. Tomorrow, we plan to _____.

10. I don't want _____.

11. You need to _____.

12. On Friday, they are _____.

13. On Mondays, we always _____.

14. She is frightened of _____.

15. He always thinks about _____.

16. She will share _____.

17. Open the window so _____.

18. We're late for _____.

19. The flowers need _____.

20. I am so tired of _____.

21. The clothes are _____.

22. I've been waiting to _____.

23. These shoes are _____.

24. How much does _____?

25. I will walk _____.

26. Remember to get _____.

27. Go call the _____.

28. It's too late to _____.

29. The baby has _____.

30. That looks like _____.

31. Yesterday we decided _____.

32. The house is _____.

33. Talk to the doctor about _____.

34. This food tastes _____.

35. Many years ago, we _____.

The Source for Aphasia Therapy

36. Go put that over _____.

37. Outside the gate, I saw _____.

38. The door was _____.

39. You were late for _____.

40. The man started _____.

41. My watch has _____.

42. There hasn't been _____.

43. The car sounded like _____.

44. Together, we made _____.

45. I called _____.

46. Don't talk about _____.

47. I don't know why _____.

48. She got mad about _____.

49. I get worried when _____.

50. I feel pain in _____.

51. Turn on _____.

52. The TV needs _____.

53. It's so cold _____.

54. I didn't make _____.

55. Did you take _____?

56. I'm sorry about _____.

57. The medicine made me _____.

58. We saw water coming _____.

59. Stop putting _____.

60. I've been watching _____.

61. The taxi driver took us _____.

62. These pants feel _____.

63. The store will _____.

64. I am out of _____.

65. The nurse said that _____.

66. I remember when _____.

67. Show us the _____.

68. The carpet has _____.

69. My friend came to _____.

70. The plate is _____.

71. Go out and _____.

72. That is just _____.

73. Take me to see _____.

74. Yesterday was _____.

75. Tomorrow will be _____.

76. The children are _____.

77. I am so happy to _____.

78. They spoke to me about _____.

79. Turn this way so _____.

80. My physical therapist makes me _____.

81. She gave me a gift for _____.

82. My ring was _____.

83. The TV show will _____.

84. Come help me _____.

85. I just can't _____.

86. The table was _____.

87. The button fell _____.

88. My hair has _____.

89. The ice was _____.

90. I am almost finished with _____.

91. Go to the closet and _____.

92. The flower pot _____.

93. The newspaper hasn't _____.

94. Put your shoes _____.

95. She gave me a big _____.

96. My teeth _____.

97. The store is _____.

98. My dog needs _____.

99. Next month, I need to _____.

100. The kids have gone _____.

Situational Sentences

Goal: The client will increase verbal expression to 80% accuracy while forming sentences.

Instructions: Ask the client to listen as you read a short situation. Have him respond with a short sentence. The goal is to begin reducing external cueing and to move toward independent cueing and/or independent verbal expression. Don't worry if the client doesn't match the given answer exactly. Accept any answer that makes sense and is an actual sentence.

Compensatory Strategies:
- Show him the cue situation and the answer *only* if it helps him produce an appropriate verbal response.
- Point to the words as the client attempts to say them.
- Beat on the table rhythmically as you point to the words.

Activity: Read each situation to the client and have him give an appropriate answer.

1. You are in a hospital room and it is time for your pain medication. You press the call button and say,

   I need my pain medicine.

2. You are sitting in a wheelchair out in the hallway of the rehabilitation center. You would like to see your nurse, but you aren't strong enough to wheel the chair all the way down to the nurse's station. A young man passes by and you say,

   Please push my chair down to the nurse's station.

3. You are awakened in your hospital bed in the middle of the night. You are cold. You press the call button to say,

   Can I have another blanket, please?

4. You are sitting in a hospital room. Your mouth is dry and your stomach begins to rumble. You press the call button to say,

   I want something to drink and to eat.

5. You have just completed physical therapy. You are exhausted and need to take a nap. You look at your therapist and say,

   Please put me in my bed.

6. You reach over to turn on your bedside lamp and the bulb is burned out. To your spouse, you say,

   The bulb in my lamp is burned out.

7. You notice that a green plant in your room has wilted. When the nursing assistant walks in your room, you say,

   Please, water my plant.

8. While you are dressing one morning, you notice that a button has fallen off your shirt. You go to your daughter to say,

   I need a button for my shirt.

9. You wake up one morning to discover that your left leg is red and swollen. It is also quite painful. You call the nurse to say,

   I feel pain in my leg.

10. You are ready for your morning grooming rituals. When you get to the sink, you discover that your comb is missing. You press the call light to say,

    Help me find my comb.

11. You are tired of being in a hospital room. You've been told that your family can now take you on short outings. When your daughter arrives, you say,

    Let's go for a ride.

12. You'd like to watch TV in your room. When you try to turn on the TV, nothing happens. You gain the attention of a nurse's aide to say,

    Please turn on the TV. (or) Please fix the TV.

13. You don't have a telephone in your room. You go to the nurse's station because you would like to make a call. When you arrive at the nurse's station, you say,

    I need to use the phone. (or) I need to write a note.

14. You want to write a note to yourself about when your daughter will be picking you up for a doctor's appointment. You approach the activities director and say,

    I need a pen or a pencil. (or) I need to write a note.

15. When you get cereal with milk for breakfast, you realize the milk is spoiled. You see a nurse's aide and say,

    The milk tastes very bad.

16. You suffer from seasonal allergies. The pollen count is quite high and you have been sneezing all day. You let out a sneeze in front of the physical therapist. Then you say,

    I need a tissue.

17. You wake up one morning and you're unsure what day and date it is. When the nursing assistant walks in the room, you say,

    What is the day and date?

18. You sit down to eat your lunch. Soup is being served, and you don't have a spoon. When the dining room attendant walks by, you say,

    Please get me a spoon.

19. At dinner one night, you notice that you don't have a napkin. To the dining room attendant, you say,

   Please get me a napkin.

20. You get black coffee at breakfast one morning. You never drink your coffee black. After the dining room attendant pours the coffee, you say,

   I need cream and sugar, please.

21. Your food doesn't have much taste. You would like to make it taste better, so you say to someone at your table,

   Please pass the salt and/or pepper.

22. You go to an ice-cream parlor on a day trip and you'd like one scoop of ice cream on a cone. It is your turn to give your order. You say,

   I'd like a single scoop of ice cream on a cone, please.

23. You'd like a small amount of money each week to buy snacks and magazines at your retirement community. Your son takes care of all your finances now. To your son, you say,

   I'd like a little pocket money, please.

24. You would like to get out of your hospital bed to sit in a chair. But you need assistance transferring your body from the bed to the chair. You press the nurse's call light to say,

   Please help me get out of bed to sit in a chair.

25. You enjoy listening to music while lying in your hospital bed. You can't reach the radio, but your roommate can. So you say,

   Please turn on the radio.

26. Your roommate enjoys watching TV. This morning, he turned on the TV with the volume extremely high. You notice that he has forgotten to place his hearing aid in his ear. So you say,

Put in your hearing aid and turn down the TV, please.

27. It has been weeks since you had a haircut. When your son arrives to visit, you say,

I need a haircut.

28. You are at the check-out counter at a local convenient store. You need an extra nickel to pay the clerk. You can't find one, so you say to your daughter,

Can I borrow a nickel, please? (or) Give the clerk a nickel, if you have one.

29. You make a batch of chocolate chip cookies during your occupational therapy session. After the cookies are out on a plate, you approach some of your new friends to say,

Would you like a cookie?

30. The telephone in your room is ringing. You can't reach the receiver from your bed. To your roommate, you say,

Please answer the phone.

31. The sun is shining too brightly through the window of your room. It's making you squint. When the nursing assistant arrives, you say,

Please pull down the blinds.

32. The housekeeping department in your retirement community has agreed to do your laundry each week. They did not pick up your clothes yesterday and you are worried that they have overlooked you. You approach the apartment manager to say,

I need my clothes washed, please.

33. You have accompanied your spouse to pick up your daughter at the airport. You are not sure about the plane's exact arrival time. You ask the gate attendant,

    What time will the plane arrive?

34. You wake up in the middle of the night smelling smoke. Your spouse is soundly sleeping. You immediately wake him up to say,

    I smell smoke.

35. You recently heard that a close friend has just lost her spouse to cancer. You'd like to send a sympathy card. To your daughter, you say,

    I want to mail a card to my friend.

36. A tire on your car went flat. You are only one mile from home. You pick up your mobile phone and dial your home number. When your spouse answers, you say,

    I have a flat tire.

37. It's dinner time and you want to wash your hands before you eat. You start to leave the dining room to do this, when a nurse stops to ask where you are going. You say,

    I'm going to wash my hands.

38. You are in a toy store trying to purchase a gift for your granddaughter's first birthday. You see a teddy bear that you know she would love. The bear is high on a shelf and out of your reach. You locate a clerk to say,

    Can you please get the bear on the high shelf for me?

39. You have received numerous floral arrangements and gifts since a recent illness. It is now time to express your thanks. You have great difficulty writing. You call your daughter to say,

    Please help me write the thank-you notes.

40. You and your spouse recently purchased a new puppy. You know your spouse always forgets things. You are worried that the puppy has not yet been taken to the vet. When your spouse comes home, you say,

    Have you taken the puppy to the vet for shots yet?

41. You enjoy playing board games. Your best friend shares this interest. You call your friend to say,

    Let's play a game at 2:00 p.m.

42. You are sitting in the kitchen while your daughter is using your recipe to make chicken pot pie. You're telling her step-by-step because the recipe is in your head and not written down. You see that your daughter is about to place the pie into a 450° oven, which is much too hot. So you say,

    Turn the oven down to 350°.

43. Your nephew wants to find out what you'd like for your birthday present. He has asked about several different items. He brings up perfume, which you are allergic to. You then say,

    Perfume always makes me sneeze. (or) I'm allergic to perfume.

44. You fell two days ago and suffered a bad break in your right arm. You now have a large cast that you'll have to wear for eight weeks. Your son asks you how long you will have to wear the cast. You say,

    I have to wear the cast on my arm for eight weeks.

45. You decide to begin a flower garden but you don't have much experience. You go to a bookstore, but you can't find the right type of book. You walk up to the clerk to say,

    Help me find a book on gardening, please.

46. Your spouse feels that you have both grown too old to take care of the yard duties. He wants to hire someone younger to cut the grass and keep the trees lopped. You agree and say,

You're right; let's hire someone to keep the yard in good shape.

47. It is time to do the weekly grocery shopping. Since your illness, you've had to ask your daughter to complete this chore. You need to tell her three more items to add to the grocery list. You say,

Please add _____, _____, and _____ to the grocery list, please.

48. You think you may have the flu and it alarms you. You know that the flu can become quite serious at your age. You make an appointment with your doctor. He asks you to describe your symptoms. You then say,

I have a fever, chills, and a bad cough.

49. You are embarrassed when you discover that you have allowed your car to run out of gas. You pull over to the side of the highway and turn on your hazard lights. A policeman arrives. With a red face, you say,

My car ran out of gas.

50. You and your spouse have planned a romantic dinner. You thought that everything was ready. Then you realize you need matches for the candles. You have no idea where the matches are in your house. To your spouse, you say,

Could you help me find the matches, dear?

Building Sentences with Cueing

Goal: The client will increase verbal expression to 90% accuracy for sentence formulation exercises with cueing.

Instructions: In this activity, you will have the client arrange words to make sentences. Photocopy the words on pages 178-180 and cut them apart into individual squares. (You can also use the words from pages 26 and 27.) Tell the client that you will select the first word, and he will need to find other words to make a complete sentence. Have him pronounce each word that he adds. After making a sentence, have him read the sentence aloud.

Compensatory Strategies:
- Enlarge the words for clients with visual difficulties.

- If you can, laminate the cards for durability. You can also glue magnets to the back of each word, and they can be placed on the side of a file cabinet or refrigerator.

- If the client struggles selecting appropriate words, then select two words and ask him to pick one that might help make the sentence. Use this dual-choice mode for all words until an appropriate sentence is made.

- Mount the words on separate index cards and cover them with clear contact paper.

- Feel free to add additional words or to customize more words to reflect your client's interests.

Activity: Photocopy the words on pages 178-180, cut them out, and place them randomly in front of the client. Start the sentence for him by picking a word and then have him add words until he makes a sentence.

a	the	all	of	under
felt	sad	last	night	clothes
drawer	book	up	shelf	walk
about	mad	lemonade	is	are
good	help	me	get	up
I	want	some	soap	dish
he	she	wants	to	eat
my	bed	needs	changing	have

new	food	bad	smoke	an
house	razor	gone	am	we
got	towel	for	coffee	hot
cold	room	feel	-s	-ing
money	was	were	pocket	will
won't	not	does	doesn't	can
today	tomorrow	towel	turn	on
off	across	down	in	at

back	neck	head	TV	visit
pass	salt	pepper	walked	went
going	they	why	what	who
that	come	how	when	where
so	from	came	give	this
yes	no	day	morning	zero
one	two	three	four	five
six	seven	eight	nine	ten

Building Sentences without Cueing

Goal: The client will increase verbal expression to 90% accuracy for sentence formulation without cueing.

Instructions: Tell the client you'll *verbally* give him a word and that he must add words until he makes a sentence. Explain that his sentence can be about anything, as long as it makes sense. Use the word list from the previous activity for your target words.

Compensatory Strategies:

- You can play a variation of this activity. You come up with one word, then the client comes up with one. Then you come up with another one, then he does, etc.

- Experiment with three word sentences and build up to longer ones if the client is able.

- Do not provide further cueing. The client should be striving for a maximum level of independence at this point in therapy.

Activity: Verbally give the client a word from the previous activity's list and have him make up his own sentence.

Goal: The client will increase sentence formulation skills to 90% accuracy at the level of conversational speech.

Instructions: In this activity, you are slowly moving from making sentences to making conversation. You will introduce the client to a number of conversational topics—descriptions, interviews, and "what if" situations. Each section has its own instructions. Feel free to add any personal items to the list to customize your therapy.

Compensatory Strategies:
- Don't put too much pressure on the client. Speech will usually flow easily from an aphasic client if he "forgets" he's speaking. Also remind people speaking with the client to be patient with his speaking ability.

- At this level, the client should be very self-directed. He should be independent or nearly independent from cueing strategies used previously during therapy. If not, go back and repeat some earlier exercises.

- Use effective distraction techniques successful in reducing anxiety the client experiences.

- Be patient, positive, and encouraging.

Activity: Use the topics in this activity as a springboard to having conversations with the client.

Descriptions
Ask the client to describe the following items in detail:

1. a car
2. a pet
3. a coat
4. a house/apartment/condo
5. his room
6. his hometown
7. his favorite restaurant
8. a particular outfit
9. a certain person
10. his mother
11. his father
12. his brother/sister
13. his backyard
14. his spouse
15. his watch

Interviews

Expand on these topics by discussing appropriate questions prior to the interview. You may want to have the client interview only you, or just other staff members if he is open to this.

1. cost of living
2. military conflicts/war
3. taxes
4. weather
5. child care
6. using credit cards
7. the environment and its protection
8. jobs
9. educational trends
10. sports
11. current events
12. marriage and divorce
13. changes in health care
14. new technology (computers, E-mail, cell phones, etc.)
15. volunteerism

"What If" Situations

Ask the client to imagine what his life would be like if these things occurred. Start out the conversation with, "What would your life be like if . . . "

1. . . . you were famous?
2. . . . you won ten million dollars?
3. . . . you lived in a foreign country?
4. . . . you experienced a war in your country?
5. . . . you unexpectedly lost your job?
6. . . . your spouse died suddenly?
7. . . . you were diagnosed with a terminal illness?
8. . . . you sustained a spinal cord injury?
9. . . . you won a new house?
10. . . . you were the victim of a violent crime?
11. . . . you became the CEO of a major company?
12. . . . you wrote a best-selling novel?
13. . . . you were stranded in a natural disaster?
14. . . . you were President of the United States?
15. . . . you discovered the cure for the common cold?

1-10-9